Kitchens & Baths

for today & tomorrow

ideas for fabulous new kitchens & baths

Jerri Farris

**Creative Publishing
international**

MINNEAPOLIS, MINNESOTA
www.creativepub.com

Creative Publishing
international

Copyright © 2008
Creative Publishing international, Inc.
400 First Avenue North
Suite 300
Minneapolis, Minnesota 55401
1-800-328-3895
www.creativepub.com

Printed in Singapore

10 9 8 7 6 5 4 3 2

Kitchens & Baths for Today & Tomorrow

Library of Congress Cataloging-in-Publication Data

Farris, Jerri.
  Kitchens & baths for today & tomorrow : ideas for
fabulous new kitchens & baths / Jerri Farris.
      p. cm.
  Summary: "Includes insider tips, do-it-yourself instructions and inspirational photos for kitchens and
bathrooms"--Provided by publisher.
  ISBN-13: 978-1-58923-374-4 (soft cover)
  ISBN-10: 1-58923-374-3 (soft cover)
  1. Kitchens--Design and construction. 2. Bath-
rooms--Design and construction. I. Title. II. Title:
Kitchens and baths for today and tomorrow.

  TX653.F34 2008
  643'.3--dc22

2007046294

President/CEO: Ken Fund
Vice President for Sales & Marketing: Kevin Hamric

Home Improvement Group

Publisher: Bryan Trandem

Managing Editor: Tracy Stanley
Senior Editor: Mark Johanson
Editor: Jennifer Gehlhar

Creative Director: Michele Lanci-Altomare
Senior Design Manager: Brad Springer
Design Managers: Mary Rohl, Jon Simpson
Page Layout Artist: Kari Johnston

Production Managers: Linda Halls, Laura Hokkanen

Author: Jerri Farris

Cover: (top): photo courtesy of SieMatic;
 (lower): photo iStock/www.istock.com

Table of Contents

5   **Introduction**

7   **DREAM KITCHENS**

15   Walls, Floors & Ceilings

35   Storage & Display

63   Food Prep & Cleanup

89   Dining & Hospitality

107   Lighting

121   Convenience & Communication

133   **DREAM BATHROOMS**

141   Walls, Floors & Ceilings

165   Storage & Display

189   Fixtures

225   Fittings

237   Lighting & Ventilation

251   Accessories

264   Resource Guide

284   Index

Introduction

Kitchens & Baths for Today & Tomorrow covers every element you need to consider when designing and remodeling or planning and decorating your kitchen or bathroom, from walls, floors and ceilings to lighting. In each chapter, you'll find several features, each of which contains a specific type of wisdom.

DesignWise features hints and tips—insider tricks—from professional kitchen planners.

DollarWise describes money-saving ideas that can be adapted to your own plans and circumstances.

IdeaWise illustrates a clever do-it-yourself project for each topic.

Some chapters also include *Words to the Wise*, a glossary of terms that may not be familiar to you. Another important feature of this book is the Resource Guide starting on page 264. This guide contains as much information as possible about most of the photographs in the book, including contact information for designers and manufacturers.

DesignWise

James R. Dase,
CKD, CBD
Abruzzo Kitchens
Schaumburg, IL

• The right sink improves the flow of work. Sinks with one extra-large basin and one smaller basin give you an area for cleaning or soaking large items and another to use in the meantime. Installing the garbage disposal in the larger basin gives you a larger space to clean heavily soiled items. A basin rack on the floor of the sink protects the surface from scratches and dents.

• Faucets with pull-out spray heads are great for easy sink cleanups and for filling large stockpots on the counter.

• To make cleanup easier, position a pull-out waste receptacle below the chopping area. If you compost organic materials, choose a small, easy-to-clean receptacle. Make sure the kitchen includes at least two pull-out waste receptacles, one for trash and one for recycling.

• Keep frequently used spices near the cooktop, in racks on a nearby wall cabinet door, or in a drawer with special inserts. To retain freshness, keep spice refills away from the heat of the cooking center.

DollarWise

If you want the look of natural stone but can't afford to do the entire floor, mix a stone tile with a similar-looking ceramic tile or use stone tiles as an accent for a ceramic tile floor.

IdeaWise

According to DeWitt Talmadge Beall, of DeWitt Designer Kitchens, a skylight is the best thing you can do for a ceiling. But what if your kitchen has a second story above it?

No problem: Create a faux skylight. Box out an inverted well, install lighting, and cover the well with sandblasted or obscured glass.

Words to the Wise

What's the difference between *framed* and *frameless* cabinets?

• On *framed cabinets*, the exposed edges of the boxes are covered with flat (face) frames. The doors may be set into the frames or overlay them; the hinges are attached to the frames and the doors.

• On *frameless cabinets*, the exposed edges of the box are covered with edge banding and the doors cover nearly the entire case. The door hinges are attached to the doors and the sides or ends of the boxes.

Which is better?

That's a matter of personal preference. Compare costs on individual styles carefully. Framed cabinets require more materials but often are less exacting to build than frameless. Conversely, frameless cabinets require less material but can be time consuming to build. The structure of frameless cabinets allows for wider doors and better accessibility, but the traditional appearance of framed cabinets is preferable in historic or traditional-style homes. As you shop, remember that door and hardware styles will be dictated to some degree by the frame style you select.

Dream Kitchens

So, you're dreaming of a dream kitchen. You're not alone, you know. Slightly more than one in four homeowners have the same kind of dream.

It's not surprising. Today's kitchens serve more roles than ever before: cooking area, dining space, home office, entertainment center. Newer homes are built to fit modern lifestyles, but more than half of the houses in America are 30 years old or older; many older kitchens simply don't measure up. Yours may be one of them. Or maybe you have a newer kitchen that just doesn't meet your needs.

It doesn't really matter why you want a new kitchen. This book can help point you in the right direction. We'll take you on a tour of more than a hundred kitchens, pointing out ideas and details that may not have occurred to you. Along the way, we're going to define a few industry terms, describe ways you can get the most for your money, give you insider tips from certified kitchen designers, and suggest specific, doable project ideas.

Cooking and sharing food has long been central to family life, a ritual that has traditionally made the kitchen the most important room in the house. The turn of the century brought us life-at-the-speed-of-light, but no matter how tech-savvy we become, nothing can replace the welcoming embrace of a fragrant kitchen or the restorative power of an hour around a table together.

Yes, meals are and will always be important, but cooking itself has become optional. "Home meal replacements" are the biggest things in the grocery industry, and "to-go" is the byword of hundreds of reasonably-priced restaurants. Kitchens remain the foundation of family life, because whether we cook a lot or not, the kitchen is where we live, where we gather, where most of us start and end our days.

Kitchens dominate our homes and therefore the remodeling landscape: There's money in them. Estimates vary by region, but a minor kitchen remodeling project returns somewhere between 78 and 98 percent of its cost in added home value, and a major remodel returns between 72 and 121 percent on resale. That's right. You and your family get to enjoy the new kitchen, and if you sell the house, you get most or all of your money back. The lucky ones among us may even turn a profit. Now, that's a win/win situation.

Careful planning

helped transform this
dowdy kitchen into a
dream come true (see
below right).

Remodeling your kitchen is a big investment in every way—time, money, and energy. Veterans of the process say it's sometimes stressful and challenging. Most also say the results are worth the effort. We can help you make the process less challenging, and here's the secret: Plan...plan...plan.

Long before saws start to whine and dust starts to fly, make a scrapbook of articles and notes on kitchens and kitchen features that interest you and photographs of kitchens you like.

Next, gather the whole family for a discussion of the project. Talk about who uses your current kitchen and how, and discuss the conveniences you'd like to have in the new version. Look through the scrapbook and work together to create a description of your collective dream kitchen. Finally, decide on a budget for the project.

If you're using a contractor or kitchen designer for your project, your scrapbook, description, and budget will be invaluable as you work together. Be sure to bring them to your meetings.

Before you finalize any plans, spend some time considering your needs and wants. Evaluate how and when you cook, where you serve meals and to whom, how often you entertain. Inventory your dishes, silverware, serving pieces, cookware, and linens, and make sure there will be places for all of it. Understanding how you use your kitchen will help you invest your remodeling dollars wisely.

Oh, one more thing: No matter how much time you budget for a remodeling project, it usually takes longer than you think. Your family needs to eat in the meantime. Before you get started, make arrangements to store, heat, and clean up enough to keep body and soul together until the kitchen's back on-line. If you're undertaking a major remodel, having the basics available somewhere else in the house—at least a bar refrigerator, a microwave, and a utility sink—just might save your sanity.

How to Use This Section

The pages that follow are packed with images of interesting, attractive, and efficient kitchens. And although we hope you enjoy looking at them, they're more than pretty pictures: they're inspiration accompanied by descriptions, facts, and details meant to help you plan your kitchen project wisely.

Some of the kitchens you see here will suit your sense of style, while others may not appeal to you at all. If you're serious about remodeling or building a kitchen, read every page—there's as much to learn in what you don't like as in what you do. Look at each photograph carefully and take notes. The details you gather are the seeds from which ideas for your new kitchen will sprout.

CHAPTER 1

Walls, Floors & Ceilings

Ask most people about remodeling their kitchen, and they'll start talking about new appliances they'd like to have or maybe the new cabinets and countertops they dream of. Those are, after all, the most obvious parts of a kitchen remodeling project. But before the appliances, before the cabinets—before anything else—you need walls, floors, and ceilings.

At first, walls, floors, and ceilings may not sound terribly exciting, but think again. As the largest surfaces in the room, they set the stage for everything else, and they have a major impact on the way your kitchen functions as well as the way it looks.

Right now you may be saying, "Walls? Floors? How could they affect the way a kitchen works?" Easy. Wall space supports cabinets, so more wall space makes more cabinets possible. In the right circumstances, a pass-through streamlines serving and cleaning up. Warmed or cushioned floors make standing more comfortable. Easy-care floors simplify maintenance. Each element is an important part of the whole.

In new construction or major remodeling projects, decisions about walls, floors, and ceilings have to be made long before cabinets are chosen, plumbing is roughed in, or electrical and lighting plans are developed. You can wait to pick most final finishes, but structural decisions, such as choosing subfloor materials, planning additional support for some types of flooring, and deciding whether or not to have soffits, have to be made early in the process.

The number of possibilities for floor and wall coverings can absolutely make your head spin. This chapter will introduce you to some of those possibilities and give you ideas that can guide your selection processes.

Walls

Walls might seem mundane—after all, most kitchens are constructed with simple drywall covered with paint or wallcovering. But after some thought, you'll find that there are more interesting options, including some that give rooms a more architectural quality. The more architectural finishes—brick, wood paneling, and so on—have to be selected before the cabinets and trim.

These homeowners are lucky to have a kitchen with such great natural structure, right? Wrong. Richness and texture were layered on in a remodeling project, the result of good design, not luck.

You certainly can't tell at first glance, but this kitchen is on the first story of a two-story home. Not exactly conducive to skylights. No problem. Good design to the rescue: A faux skylight floods the room with light.

The home's ordinary drywall walls and ceilings were no barrier to good design either. Cladding walls with real face brick added substance and texture. Installing reclaimed barn wood beams injected aged textures and colors. Speaking of colors, the bricks were painted white to brighten the other earth tones of the room, but in another color scheme, they could easily have been left natural.

Wood variations from the floor are mimicked on the island and kitchen countertops for a cohesive design.

Special panels match the dishwasher to the cabinet doors.

The backsplash is the most significant part of a kitchen wall. This is the place to play with color, texture, and light.

Multi-colored subway tiles perk up the neutral color palette of this tiny kitchen. When you incorporate subtle variations like this, don't make them compete for attention with loads of other details. Light them well and let them shine.

Make the backsplash the focal point of the cooking center by adding a tile medallion or mural. Tile manufacturers offer such features, but it's easy to create one by arranging trim and other specialty tiles in a custom design. Draw full-size plans on brown paper and tape your favorite in place for a day or two before committing. You may surprise yourself with your creativity.

Ceramic tile and kitchens go together like peanut butter and jelly. Impervious to water and stains, durable, and reasonably priced—tile backsplashes are attractive, easy to maintain, and affordable. This backsplash mixes textures and colors to make a strong but subtle statement.

Stainless steel makes an ideal backsplash behind a cooktop. It's watertight, heat resistant, easy to clean, and incredibly durable. In this kitchen, brushed stainless steel protects the walls behind the range and provides a softly reflective surface that contrasts nicely with the countertops. Stainless steel receptacle plates complete the wall's tailored appearance.

Wood—especially in the form of beadboard— makes an excellent wallcovering in a kitchen. It's most practical in areas that won't be exposed to a lot of water or grease, but if you protect it with paint or sealer, wood even works as a backsplash behind sinks or in cooking areas.

Beadboard panels in the door fronts coordinate with the beadboard on the walls.

Solid-surface material is available in ¼"-thick sheets for use as wall panels and backsplashes. In this kitchen, the green backsplash is detailed with a white stripe to coordinate it with the banded countertops.

Strong color generates interest.

Cherry red demands attention, warming the white subway-style ceramic tile walls. By mixing white tile and painted cabinets with deep color and stainless accents, the homeowners created the illusion of depth within a relatively small space.

Cladding the cooking center walls with real face brick warmed and mellowed this brand new kitchen, adding to its Old World feel.

Tight quarters can leave kitchens feeling gloomy. Not in this kitchen! By painting the walls and concentrating vivid color on the cabinets and rugs, these homeowners defined their kitchen as a warm, cozy space.

Floors

Glance around a kitchen. What do you see first? Chances are, your brain takes in the cabinets, the counters and backsplash, and then. . .the floor. That's right. The floor. It's typically the largest horizontal surface in the room and undeniably the most used. It's important to choose flooring that fits your taste, lifestyle, and budget.

Bamboo floors work wonderfully in kitchens. Flat grains and natural colors like this are particularly well suited to contemporary kitchens.

The kitchen is a natural dividing line for changing from one floor covering to another. Make sure there's enough contrast that the difference looks intentional. Too close and they could look like a jacket and pants that aren't the same, but also not different enough to go together.

Tile is a durable flooring that lets you achieve a unique, customized look without spending a fortune. In this traditional kitchen, homeowners combined large and small, white and black tiles to create an interesting but subtle background.

Borders give this floor zip.

Flooring Options

Each type of flooring has unique characteristics and installation techniques. Appearance is important, but so are durability, ease-of-care, installation requirements, and environmental impact.

Hardwood

Hardwood floors look and feel warm, are durable, and are easy to clean. True, they can be scratched or dented and need periodic refinishing, but they don't develop wear patterns and can last a lifetime or two. Installation techniques vary.

Tongue-and-groove strip flooring is installed using a power nailer.

Parquet and end grain floors are set in adhesive.

Floating floors are fastened at the tongue-and-groove connections only.

Laminates

Laminate flooring consists of thin layers of plastic laminate bonded to a fiberboard core. It resists scratches and heavy traffic, and is easy to clean. If you're going to install it yourself, remember that it requires a perfectly smooth subfloor.

Laminate flooring is installed like a floating hardwood floor.

Bamboo

Bamboo flooring is durable, attractive, and environmentally sound. Bamboo is actually a grass, and although harvested every three to five years, it continues to regenerate.

Bamboo is installed using the techniques for tongue-and-groove hardwood flooring.

Cork

Cork is comfortable to walk on, easy to clean, and environmentally friendly. The bark of a cork oak tree naturally splits every 9 to 15 years and can be harvested many times without harming the tree.

Cork planks are installed like tongue-and-groove hardwood.

Cork tile is installed with adhesive, similar to parquet flooring.

Vinyl

Inexpensive, easy to clean, and durable, vinyl flooring is available in a huge variety of colors.

Sheet vinyl with felt backing is glued to the subfloor.

Sheet vinyl with PVC backing is glued only along the edges, called perimeter-bond.

Vinyl tiles typically come in 12 or 16" squares and are available with or without self-adhesive backing.

Ceramic Tile

The basic categories are:

Glazed ceramic tile: coated with glaze after it's baked, then fired again to produce a hard surface.

Porcelain tile: extremely dense and hard, and naturally water resistant. Its color runs throughout its thickness.

Quarry tile: unglazed, porous tile that's softer and thicker than glazed tile. It needs to be sealed periodically.

All ceramic tile flooring is installed with the same basic process: set the tile in thin-set mortar, then grout it. It's very doable, but requires time for planning and for the step-by-step process.

Natural Stone Tile

Granite, marble, and slate tiles are the most common stone products for floors. Granite and marble are generally sold with polished or sealed surfaces. Slate tiles, formed by cleaving the stone along natural faults, have textured surfaces.

Natural stone is installed like ceramic tile. The materials and installation are quite expensive. You may be able to find discounts on the stone, but don't skimp when it comes to installation materials.

Resilient flooring typically is the least expensive kitchen flooring material, as well as the simplest and quickest to install. If the price, easy installation, and simple maintenance appeal to you, but not the traditional patterns, look again. Today's sheet vinyl introduces the look of more costly floor coverings at more reasonable prices.

Plank-flooring-patterned sheet vinyl graces the floor of this fabulous farm-style kitchen.

Accent squares in the flooring coordinate with the counters and backsplash.

The resilient flooring in this elegant kitchen mimics the look of ceramic tile.

The warmth, beauty, and availability of hardwood flooring make it very popular in North American kitchens, especially in the East and Midwest. Solid wood flooring is relatively expensive, but with the right finishes, it's durable and needs only frequent vacuuming and occasional damp mopping to look its best. Although wood can be scratched and dented, it also can be returned to its original glory with periodic refinishing, a factor that makes it cost effective over time.

Plank hardwood flooring complements the rustic look of this kitchen. The color variations of the planks go well with the unusual drawer fronts.

Strip hardwood floors blend well in many styles of kitchens. The warm tones of this hardwood floor provide a lovely background for this large kitchen and adjoining living room.

Laminate flooring is available in many colors and textures. You can choose from patterns designed to replicate the look of materials as diverse as hardwood, ceramic tile, and even concrete.

Laminate flooring resists scratches and heavy wear from traffic, and it's easy to maintain with light cleaning. Wood patterns are common, but not the only options.

Cork—either vinyl-coated or waxed—is resilient, impervious to water and insects, and easy on the knees and feet. In this kitchen, cork flooring in a checkerboard pattern repeats the natural-and-black combination used throughout the room.

Design Wise

DeWitt Talmadge Beall

DeWitt Designer Kitchens
Studio City, CA

Simplicity gives a design power. Try these ideas:

Floors

• Choose a floor covering that reflects the color of the cabinets or the counters/backsplash.

• Consider installing radiant heating mats under stone or tile. They make a hard floor more friendly and are an efficient source of heat.

• Continuous floors are good, but be careful with natural hardwood running into laundry areas. Prevent water damage by installing a sheet metal washer tray that includes its own drain.

Walls

• Take a stone or tile backsplash to the ceiling behind a range or cooktop and float a hood against it.

• Clad sections of the wall in panels to match the cabinetry, and float shelves or rail systems against it.

Ceilings

• Skylights are the best thing you can do for a ceiling. Choose units that can be opened and closed with remote controls, feature Low-E glass, and have several modes of light control.

• Uplight the ceiling with dimmable xenon lights placed on the tops of wall cabinets set approximately 15" from the ceiling. Position the lights forward behind the crown for maximum dispersion and to eliminate hot spots on the walls.

Ceilings

Compared to other elements in the kitchen, the choices for ceiling surfaces are relatively limited. In most kitchens, the ceilings are constructed with a drywall base and covered with paint or wallcovering. Those are the most common but not the only alternatives, of course. For something different, try plaster, a mural, painted or stained beadboard, wood panels, or decorative beams.

Soaring white ceiling, white walls, white cabinets, white counters, white floors.

So what makes this space feel vibrant rather than like the inside of a refrigerator? Creativity, innovation, and color.

Start with the flying cornice bridge. This unusual structure wraps the room with color, defining the space without closing it off. Although it's sophisticated, the bridge isn't complicated. The ends rest on the cabinets and the center is supported by polished metal rods anchored in the ceiling.

Next, the remarkable backsplash. Made entirely of glass, the etched glass design is lit from below by a neon tube running through a channel.

And don't forget the floor. Framed by a toekick and the transition to the adjacent flooring, color warms this white tile floor.

If you decide to add details to a ceiling, make sure the style, shape, size, and color are well suited to the room.

Creativity, innovation, and color.

The rustic beams accenting the ceiling of this southwestern kitchen add a sort of sunbleached authenticity to the room.

Here, rustic wood beams define the high, peaked ceiling. The paneling pays tribute to the homeowners' Scandinavian heritage.

Extra details make ornamental beams look more architectural. Sandwiched between cove molding and another line of trim molding, bearing blocks provide substance to these decorative beams.

Light fixtures recessed into the beams lighten and brighten the room.

IdeaWise

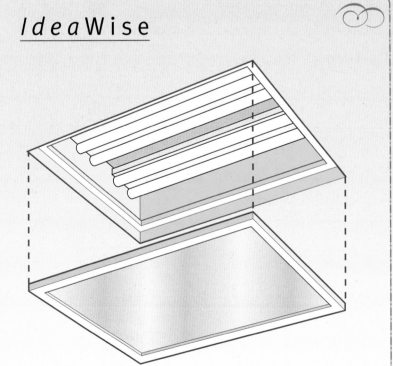

According to DeWitt Talmadge Beall, of DeWitt Designer Kitchens, a skylight is the best thing you can do for a ceiling. But what if your kitchen has a second story above it?

No problem: Create a faux skylight. Box out an inverted well, install lighting, and cover the well with sandblasted or obscured glass.

Layer on the details.

Paneling, beams, and posts
give character to new construction.

Drywall and paint might have been too little. A variety of coverings might have been too much. But like Goldilocks, these homeowners found a solution that was just right. Pine sheathing covers the walls and ceilings, unifying the various angles and planes of the room without camouflaging them.

Look carefully at the points where the walls and ceiling meet: The planks are matched up with the precision of a hand-tailored pinstriped suit. This kind of attention to detail marks the difference between the work of a craftsman and an amateur.

If you decide to do something like this in your own kitchen, plan, plan, plan. Measure, calculate, and make detailed drawings before you make the first cut. The time you invest in planning will pay off in a professional-looking job.

CHAPTER 2

Storage & Display

Let's face it: cabinets make or break a kitchen. They establish how the room looks, and how it works. The style of the room, its color scheme, traffic patterns, level of convenience—they all start with the cabinets. And if you're building or doing a major remodel, one more thing needs to start there: the budget. Cabinets represent the single largest investment in a typical kitchen.

If your current cabinets provide enough storage, but you just don't like the way they look, consider painting or refacing them. Painting in an option only for wood cabinets, but both wood and laminate cabinets can be refaced by installing new cabinet doors, drawer fronts, and matching veneer for covering face frames and cabinet ends. Refacing costs more than painting but much less than installing all new cabinets.

If you decide to go all the way, do it right. Make a budget, evaluate your real needs and wants, and learn as much as you can about cabinet design and construction, especially if you're working on your own. If you're using a kitchen designer or contractor, you can rely on their knowledge and experience, but you still need to be prepared to make wise choices. At the end of the day, you're the one who's going to be living with these decisions—and paying for them.

Start your research right here. This chapter is filled with information, ideas, and photographs of attractive, interesting, efficient kitchens. Take notes and have fun.

Cabinets

The next few pages will introduce you to ready-to-assemble (RTA), stock, semi-custom, and custom cabinetry. Learn as much as you can about each option so you can fairly evaluate quality, price, and durability as well as the available styles and finishes. Once you've decided on a type and style, take advantage of every resource available to you when it comes to designing the cabinet layout. As we've said, you're likely to live with this choice for a long time.

Ready-to-assemble (RTA) cabinets are available through home centers and furnishings retailers. The cases are standard, but you select the style of doors, end panels, and accessories you want to include. You need to measure your kitchen and create a plan, but most stores offer in-store kitchen designers who will review your layout and give you hints and options.

Several retailers offer kitchen planning guides, including downloadable kitchen planning tools, that let you try out various configurations within the dimensions of your kitchen.

Words to the Wise

What's the difference between *framed* and *frameless* cabinets?

• On **framed cabinets,** the exposed edges of the boxes are covered with flat (face) frames. The doors may be set into the frames or overlay them; the hinges are attached to the frames and the doors.

• On **frameless cabinets,** the exposed edges of the box are covered with edge banding and the doors cover nearly the entire case. The door hinges are attached to the doors and the sides or ends of the boxes.

Which is better?

That's a matter of personal preference. Compare costs on individual styles carefully. Framed cabinets require more materials but often are less exacting to build than frameless. Conversely, frameless cabinets require less material but can be time consuming to build. The structure of frameless cabinets allows for wider doors and better accessibility, but the traditional appearance of framed cabinets is preferable in historic or traditional-style homes. As you shop, remember that door and hardware styles will be dictated to some degree by the frame style you select.

Stock cabinets,
available through home
centers, are offered in a
range of standard sizes,
usually in 3" increments.
A limited variety of door
styles and colors can be
purchased off the shelf or
delivered within a few
days. Some specialized
accessories or units may
have to be special ordered.
You can install them
yourself, take advantage
of the installation services
offered through the home
center, or hire a carpenter.

Semi-custom cabinets
are manufactured in hundreds
of standard sizes, finishes and
styles. You can buy these
cabinets through home
centers, kitchen designers,
and contractors.

Following a plan that you
or you and a designer have
created, your cabinets are
built to order according to
the manufacturer's standard
specifications. You can install
the cabinets yourself, use the
installation services offered
through the home center,
hire a carpenter, or have your
contractor install them.

Custom cabinets can be built by a custom manufacturer or by a cabinet shop. In either case, you get—and pay for—high-quality materials and workmanship, practically an infinite number of details, accessories, and sizes, and specialized styling. Custom cabinets are typically installed by a contractor or by the cabinetmakers themselves.

Guidelines from the National Kitchen and Bath Association recommend that every kitchen includes at least five storage or organizing items located between 15 and 48" above the finished floor. Cabinets of every kind—from RTA to custom—can be outfitted with accessories to organize and store kitchen utensils. Of course, the price of the cabinets goes up with every built-in convenience. Fortunately, many accessories are available as add-ons, so you can continue to accessorize your cabinets over time.

Before you order new cabinets, investigate accessory options. Retail stores, catalogs, and Internet sites devoted to organization typically offer a wide variety of cabinet accessories. Compare features and prices of built-in accessories to add-ons of similar quality, and create a plan that offers the most convenience possible within your budget.

Remember that add-on accessories have to be installed. That's not an issue if you're doing the work yourself, but if you're hiring someone to do it, be sure to factor the cost of installation into the comparison between built-ins and add-ons.

Spice drawers are handy when you're baking—individual bottles can be identified and selected easily.

These slide-out drawers have heavy-duty runners with special guides for side stability. The plate rack as well as the lid holder are made of solid beech and aluminum. The sturdiness and stability of these drawers make them easy to use and reliable for many years.

Pullout shelves take advantage of otherwise wasted space. Here, an instant liquor cabinet is within reach behind a built-in bench.

Expanding shelves bring the contents of the corner out to you.

Roll-out shelves improve the efficiency of nearly every cabinet, from large pantries to narrow tray cabinets. Plan carefully and invest wisely. There are few things more frustrating in a kitchen than flimsy, poorly supported shelves and glides that don't work smoothly.

Revolving corner systems are efficient and affordable.

Try looking at corners from a different angle.

The corner. You know the story—nothing but wasted space, awkward angles, and traffic tie-ups. Forget all that. Handled with care, corners become usable, attractive spaces—sometimes even the highlight of the kitchen.

Upper cabinets telescope down toward the corner,
focusing attention on the elegant windows and the magnificent view from this urban kitchen. A display shelf disguises the potentially awkward gap at the back, and an angled double-bowl sink nestles into the remaining space.

No soaring windows?
No problem—create your own view. Set the sink in an angled cabinet recessed from the profile of the base cabinets, and add lighted display space above. The interesting profile of this arrangement is enhanced by edge banding on the counters, island, and backsplash.

Interior lighting adds impact.

The most useful storage space is between hip and shoulder height, according to ergonomic experts. Dropping a wall cabinet all the way to the countertop, connecting the wall cabinet to the base, makes a wall cabinet work like a china cabinet. The right trim and finish can make it look like one, too.

Far from a liability, this corner became the foundation of a baking center. The base cabinet adjacent to the corner was recessed and its countertop lowered to create convenient workspace. Narrow cabinets on either side extend all the way to the countertop, framing the space; an appliance garage completes the arrangement. The recessed workspace base leaves room for the folding door and swing-out shelves of the corner unit to operate. A similar arrangement makes the space in the upper corner fully functional. Open display shelves round out the end of the cabinets.

*Design*Wise

Lori Jo Krengel, CKD, CBD

Krengel Kitchens
St. Paul, MN

• Build in storage underneath an island. This storage can also act as the countertop support.

• Use the toekick space below your cabinetry. Plan for a pull-out step stool for access to higher cabinets.

• Build around an obstruction and use the space for spices and small item storage.

• If you've fallen in love with see-through bins that display pasta, grain, and other items but can't afford to waste the space on the merely ornamental, don't worry. Place dividers 3" back in the bin, and you can use the space behind the display items.

• Booths and banquettes often include storage space under the seats, but it's often not as easily accessible as other storage areas. Reserve this space for seasonal items and specialty equipment that you need only occasionally.

Decked out with dark stain and glass doors,

an angled upper cabinet acts as an accent piece. A lighted interior

focuses attention on the items displayed there.

*Continuing the light
trim molding integrates
the display piece into
the other cabinets.*

Anxious to display as many of their treasured pieces as possible, the homeowners crafted this simple but elegant display piece. The top shelf has grooves routed into the shelf to support and stabilize the plates on display.

Denim-like textures and colors on the beadboard ceiling, backsplash tiles, and hand-painted stools set the stage for the homeowner's collection of classic and contemporary blue and white collectibles. Complementary natural tones temper the blue and warm the white of the doors and drawers of the base cabinets, countertops, and soffits. Together they create a clean, spare look that suits the rest of the house as well as the homeowner's lifestyle.

If you can't decide between a window and one more upper cabinet, choose both. Windows make dramatic backdrops for display cabinets. This cabinet has a glass panel in back and glass doors in front. The crystal and glassware inside reflect and refract sunshine, lighting up the kitchen on sunny days.

IdeaWise

Tired of a tripping over shoes in the back hall? Cap the end of a cabinet run with a low, open bench built to match. Top the bench with a cushion, and the clever storage piece becomes a convenient place to change shoes as well.

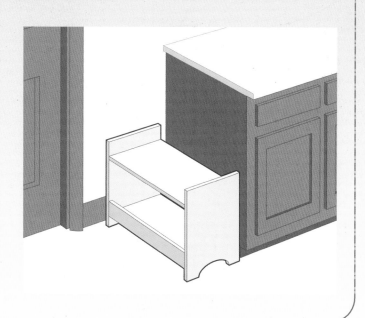

Combining finishes or colors creates an interesting, custom look.

The pine cabinetry in this kitchen is the same throughout, despite the appearance that individual sections are freestanding pieces. To create this impression, the designers used color. The base cabinets and island are one color, the wine bar a lighter version of that color, and the cabinets framing the window are a green that complements the countertops. This simple technique sets separate areas apart and coordinates them with one another without matching.

Color accentuates the positive in this traditional kitchen.

Painted trim molding matches the island and built-in display piece, focusing attention in all the right places. The white countertops on the perimeter cabinets blend into the white tile backsplash, giving the island's rich marble countertop the prominence it deserves.

Hand-painted tiles and cheerful collectibles complete this colorful picture.

Islands provide convenient space for meal preparation and informal dining as well as storage and display space.

This multi-level island is home to a sink, food preparation area, informal eating area, and a wine rack.

The raised countertop provides casual dining space and shields the sink and work spaces from view. One of the disadvantages of an open-plan kitchen is that meal preparation areas can be seen from other spaces—often from a family or great room. That's not a problem if you're a tidy cook, but most families find that there are times when a little camouflage is welcome.

The island's counter and finish match the rest of the cabinets, which keeps it from dominating the room.

A wine rack tucked under the counter supplies storage without using much floor space.

The stained shoe provides a graceful transition between the painted molding and the hardwood floor.

This one-level island provides an uninterrupted work surface as well as casual dining space. The handsomely crafted legs supporting the dining extension give the island the look of fine furniture.

Open shelves cap off the island with display space. Open shelves like this can be used to show off special accessories or to house books, especially cookbooks.

Recessed lights supply the general lighting for this kitchen, but pendants provide attractive task lighting for the island. Controlled separately by a rheostat, the pendants can be turned up while you're cooking and then dimmed for meals.

Make sure the aisles around an island remain at least 42" wide in a one-cook kitchen and at least 48" wide in a multi-cook kitchen.

This island provides most of the food preparation area in this kitchen. A small sink nestled at the end of the island provides a handy source of water for those chores.

Glass panel doors echo the window style.

Open, recessed shelves are great places to store large serving pieces or even cookware, if it's attractive.

A plate rack on the side of the island, just opposite the sink, is an unusual touch—very handy for putting plates away after a meal. The island itself is stained to match the base cabinets, but the bookshelf at the end is finished to match the uppers. Combining finishes is an easy way to get the furniture look that's so popular in today's kitchens.

Bowed cabinets soften the ends of this island. Guidelines developed by the National Kitchen and Bath Association suggest that open counter corners be clipped or cut along a radius to eliminate sharp corners. Rounding the corners of this island made them safer as well as more interesting.

If rounded corners appeal to you, consider this: MDF (medium-density fiberboard) lends itself to curves much more easily than other cabinet materials. When shopping for MDF cabinets, make sure the tops, bottoms, and sides of the cabinet cases are ⅝" or ¾" thick. Thinner materials—typically ¼"—are fine for cabinet backs, which don't support any weight, but the rest of the case needs the strength of more substantial materials.

When properly finished, MDF makes beautiful, durable cabinets, but it's important to note that water completely destroys unfinished MDF. Since many kitchen tasks start and end with water, it's absolutely mandatory that all edges and surfaces of MDF cabinets be completely covered with laminate or paint. The faces of doors and drawers on many high-quality MDF cabinets are finished with a PVC coating and paint, an excellent system.

Countertops

DollarWise

Save more expensive materials for smaller, specialty areas—marble for a baking center or stainless steel surrounding a cooktop—and install less expensive materials in others. As long as the colors and textures are complementary, combinations make kitchens more interesting.

The style and color of its countertops have tremendous impact on a kitchen's appearance, but countertop materials are more than just a pretty (sur)face. Indeed, those materials affect the way you use and clean your kitchen. With some materials, you have be careful not to stain, scratch, or scorch the surface. Others demand specific cleaning routines. Heat-resistant surfaces, such as granite, stainless steel, tile, and other solid surfaces, make it easy to transfer hot pans or dishes from range or oven.

Edge treatments also play an important part in the appearance and function of countertops. Decorative profiles, color banding, and mixed materials all create additional interest.

Generally, it's best to select your cabinets and flooring materials, then choose materials, colors, and textures for your countertops.

The National Kitchen and Bath Association guidelines suggest that every kitchen include at least two work counter heights: one at 28 to 36" above the floor, and one at 36 to 45" above the floor. The guidelines also suggest that kitchens under 150 square feet have 132" of usable counter frontage, and kitchens over 150 square feet have at least 198" of usable counter frontage. (Complete guidelines are available from the National Kitchen and Bath Association—see page 140 for further information.)

Natural stone offers a cool surface, excellent for handling dough, especially pastry.

This California contemporary-style kitchen features maple cabinets topped with maple countertops. Granite counters surround the range and extend from the island, providing excellent surfaces for food preparation and casual dining. Paired with the mellow maple of the upper counter and the aged, distressed green finish of the island, the green-gold jupurana granite is particularly appealing.

Butcher-block countertops can be scratched and can absorb stains and odors. They're resistant to heat but will burn if exposed to enough heat. You can sand and reseal the surface to repair scratches and minor damage.

To prevent warping, seal both sides of butcher-block countertops with nontoxic polyurethane. Cutting board areas, well away from water sources, can be left unsealed; just rub them periodically with mineral, tung, or linseed oil. Don't use vegetable oil, which turns rancid over time.

Granite counters have smooth, cool, heat-resistant surfaces that also resist marks and scratches, though they do absorb some oils and stains. Important point: Damaged granite counters can't be repaired—replacement is the only option.

Portuguese tile gives this countertop distinction, but the definitive touch of style comes in the edge treatment for the undermount sinks. Switching from the white tile to blue trim defines the sink areas and helps coordinate the front edge treatment with the rest of the counter as well as with the homeowner's collection of blue-and-white collectibles.

Tile is impervious to water and stains, and highly resistant to scratches. In fact, the grout is the only part of a tile countertop that's susceptible to damage from everyday wear and tear. Using epoxy grout reduces staining, mildew, and other damage on countertops and backsplashes.

This kitchen takes advantage of two fine countertop materials. The cabinets are topped with white solid-surface countertops; the island cooking area boasts black granite. This kitchen might have been bland with all white countertops or too heavy with all black. Mixing materials produced a combination of strengths and a nicely balanced look.

Granite makes excellent counters, especially for an island like this: It resists heat, marks, and scratches. Granite counters do require some care in use, though. They can absorb oils and odors, and can be damaged if subjected to enough force. Major damage is an expensive proposition because granite can't be repaired, only replaced.

Concrete countertops blend seamlessly into the decor of this sleek, spare kitchen. Smooth, heat and stain resistant, and easy to clean up, the warm, aged finish and natural look of concrete is suitable to a broad range of kitchen designs.

Pre-cast concrete countertops generally are shipped to the job site and cut to fit with a diamond blade on a skill saw, wet or dry. They also can be cast in place.

Either way, they need to be sealed with a lacquer sealer. Fabricators recommend paste waxing concrete countertops every three months and resealing them every year or two.

Most manufacturers recommend mild, non-abrasive, non-ammoniated soap for daily cleaning. Avoid abrasive soaps, pads, and cleansers.

Concrete counters are prone to cracking, but the typical hairline cracks don't affect their structural integrity. Although they can be patched, many people consider cracks part of the look of concrete counters. Stains can be removed by sanding with 100-grit sandpaper and then reapplying sealer and wax.

Stainless steel counters and backsplashes work with stainless steel appliances to make this galley kitchen as easy to look at as it is to clean. The stainless surfaces softly reflect light, making the space seem more spacious than it actually is.

When it comes to resistance to heat, water, and damage, stainless steel is the absolute champion. It lasts practically forever and, as you see here, can be formed into edging, backsplashes, and sinks. (Welding a prefabricated stainless sink into a countertop is a less expensive option than an integral sink, however.)

For sturdy countertops, use 14 or 16 gauge steel (the smaller the number, the thicker the steel) over ¼" plywood—the plywood adds strength and muffles sound. For backsplashes, 18 to 22 gauge, steel is fine.

Use mild detergent, baking soda, or vinegar diluted in water to clean stainless steel. If you are using any kind of an abrasive, clean in the direction of the grain. Never use bleach, and avoid steel wool—fine particles left in the surface will eventually rust, making it look like the stainless itself is rusting. Scratches can't be repaired, but that's not a problem—most people like the satin look they produce.

Marble tops this island baking center, just waiting for pastry to be rolled or cookies to be cut on its smooth, cool surface. Marble scratches somewhat easily, and, like granite, it isn't repairable. It's impervious to heat but absorbs oils and some odors. Because it's rather porous, it can be stained, especially by acidic foods. Seal it with a penetrating sealer every few years.

There are ways to make natural stone countertops more affordable. Research suppliers carefully—prices vary widely, depending on where the stone is quarried and dressed and how it's finished. If you need only a small piece for an island, you might find a bargain at a local stone yard. If seams are necessary, talk with your designer or contractor about how they'll be handled.

*Dollar*Wise

You can use thinner, less expensive stone for countertops without sacrificing strength or appearance. Start with a ¾"-thick slab and support it on a ¾" plywood substrate— it's less likely to deflect that way. Laminate a matching stone strip to the slab to make a more substantial edge. By combining profiles on the strip and the slab, you can create an illusion of depth and thickness.

Although thicker slabs don't need substrates, their weight does need to be adequately supported by braces, brackets, or blocking.

Solid-surface countertops are easy to restore. Light sanding will remove surface scratches, burns, and stains; more significant damage requires professional restoration. Since its introduction in the early 1970s, solid surface materials have quickly become one of the most popular counter materials on the market. They resist heat, marks, and scratches. And because the color goes all the way through the material, minor damage simply can be sanded or polished away.

Solid-surface materials easily can be cut and shaped, so interesting contours, elaborate edge profiles, and integral drainboards are possible. And again, because the material is solid, these counters can be used with undermount sinks.

Thinner solid-surface material is available for backsplashes, such as the one shown here.

Plastic laminate—available in a truly vast variety—can be found to complement virtually any decorating scheme. It works well in cooking centers like this because it doesn't absorb stains, oils, or odors. For decades, plastic laminate has been the countertop of choice in millions of homes because it's inexpensive, durable, and easy to maintain. Although the laminate itself is quite water resistant, the substrate beneath is not, so seams and sink cutouts have to be sealed thoroughly.

You have to be careful with plastic laminate countertops— they can be scratched, chipped, or scorched. But if the worst happens, it's the easiest and least expensive type of countertop material to replace.

Clean, white laminate counters blend well with this traditional kitchen decor.

Solid-core laminate may not be for everyone—it's more expensive and not available in as many colors and patterns. If you plan to use standard laminate, consider bevel-edge molding or wood or metal nosing to cover the dark line of the kraft-paper core.

CHAPTER 3

Food Prep & Cleanup

According to Craig Claiborne, "For those who love it, cooking is at once child's play and adult joy."

Even for those who love to cook—maybe especially for them—it's more fun to work in a kitchen where high-quality appliances, workspaces, and storage areas are thoughtfully arranged. Successful kitchens start with careful observation of the people who cook there—who they are and how they like to work. For example, how many people typically work in the kitchen at once? Are they right- or left-handed? Average height, taller than average, or shorter than average? What physical limitations do they have? It's only when you've answered questions like these that you're ready to begin planning the food preparation and clean-up areas of a kitchen.

If you're replacing appliances, there are other important questions to ask yourself. After all, in a typical kitchen, the investment in appliances is second only to cabinets. Start by considering how your family cooks, day to day. If most of your cooking is really just warming prepared food, sophisticated appliances may not be worth the money. On the other hand, if you don't feel you've cooked unless you've dirtied every pot and pan in the house, appliances with all the latest bells and whistles may be good investments. Only you can determine what you truly need and how much of what you want fits within your budget.

When it comes to kitchen remodeling, space needs to be budgeted as carefully as money. Large appliances and wall oven/cooktop combinations take floor and counter space that could be used in other ways—preparation areas or storage space, for example. In smaller kitchens, there are simply fewer square feet available, which means you'll need to conserve wherever possible.

Throughout this chapter, you'll find ideas and suggestions about how to create an efficient, comfortable, enjoyable kitchen.

Meal Preparation

The three basic centers of operation in any kitchen are food prep, cooking, and cleanup. The food prep areas involve the refrigerator and sink; cooking—the cooktop, oven, and microwave; cleanup—the sink, dishwasher, and recycling areas. Ideally, these centers of operations should be placed in convenient relationships to one another. The standard work triangle is a practical starting point and often leads to well-designed kitchens, but it's by no means the only way to approach the issue.

Dual sinks certainly aren't a necessity, but in multi-cook kitchens, they're practical luxuries. In this kitchen, a large two-bowl sink for food preparation and cleanup sits in the corner by the window, and a smaller food prep sink rests in the island. The deep bowl and the pull-out sprayer faucet on the food prep sink make it a handy place to clean vegetables, rinse dishes, or fill pots.

This large kitchen has another luxury—lots of counter space. Every kitchen should have a food preparation area near the sink, at least 36" of uninterrupted counter to the left of the sink for right-handed people or to the right for left-handed people. Multi-cook kitchens should include 36" of counter space for each cook.

The double wall ovens here are positioned so one or the other is at a convenient height for almost anyone. The top oven is in a convenient position for a cook of average height, but the lower one can be reached by smaller or seated persons. Plus, the ovens are adjacent to a long expanse of solid-surface countertop, perfect landing space for dishes straight out of the oven.

If you're planning to have a window like this, remember that you'll want to open it! This double-hung is within reach, but that's not always the case. If there's too much distance between you and the window, a double-hung is awkward. Casement windows, which crank open, are easy to operate as long as the handle is within reach.

With a bar stool of just the right height, a cook can comfortably sit while working— the island's height and the countertop's overhang are designed for that.

Side-by-side refrigerators, which often include through-the-door ice/ water dispensers, require less clearance for the swing of the doors than other configurations.

This sink and refrigerator are aligned with one another, with workspace between. This arrangement makes it easy to prepare and serve meals and snacks. With a minimum of steps, you can pull out milk for breakfast, wash and cut fruit for a snack, or cook a multi-course meal. With the island so well positioned in relationship to the sink and refrigerator, even cleaning up after a meal is a breeze.

When shopping for a refrigerator, take a tape measure along. Evaluate the interior space and layout as well as the door swing clearance. Don't forget to check the noise level—no one wants to listen to the refrigerator hum all evening.

The built-in refrigerator is disguised with cabinetry panel fronts to create a custom look. Built-in refrigerators are popular, but quite expensive. If a built-in refrigerator suits your taste but not your budget, check out the alternatives. Several manufacturers offer models with designer doors that give you a built-in look. They may not have quite the same custom fit, but they don't take as big a bite out of your appliance budget either.

In an interesting twist, this kitchen includes a sink in one island, a cooktop in another, and a refrigerator on a diagonal from each. Counter space located to one side of the refrigerator is especially convenient when it comes time to put away the groceries. The raised countertops surrounding each island provide good landing space and screen the work areas from view.

Bottom-freezer and top-freezer refrigerators typically are less expensive than side-by-side models. They cost less over time, too, since they're more energy efficient.

---

*Design*Wise

James R. Dase,
CKD, CBD

Abruzzo Kitchens
Schaumburg, IL

• The right sink improves the flow of work. Sinks with one extra-large basin and one smaller basin give you an area for cleaning or soaking large items and another to use in the meantime. Installing the garbage disposal in the larger basin gives you a larger space to clean heavily soiled items. A basin rack on the floor of the sink protects the surface from scratches and dents.

• Faucets with pull-out spray heads are great for easy sink cleanups and for filling large stockpots on the counter.

• To make cleanup easier, position a pull-out waste receptacle below the chopping area. If you compost organic materials, choose a small, easy-to-clean receptacle. Make sure the kitchen includes at least two pull-out waste receptacles, one for trash and one for recycling.

• Keep frequently used spices near the cooktop, in racks on a nearby wall cabinet door, or in a drawer with special inserts. To retain freshness, keep spice refills away from the heat of the cooking center.

Clean-up Center

The major elements of a clean-up center are the sink, dishwasher, and garbage/recycling area. Like the folk wisdom about real estate, when it comes to the clean-up center, the three most important factors are: location, location, and location.

Despite advances in dishwasher technology, doing the dishes still starts at the sink. To simplify the transfer of dishes and utensils, place the dishwasher within 36" of the main sink. Allow 21" of standing room on one side or the other—both if you can. If doing the dishes is a group effort at your house, make sure more than one person can reach the dishwasher at a time.

The quality of a stainless steel sink is measured by the thickness of the steel, the amount of chromium and nickel it contains, and the effectiveness of the sound control.

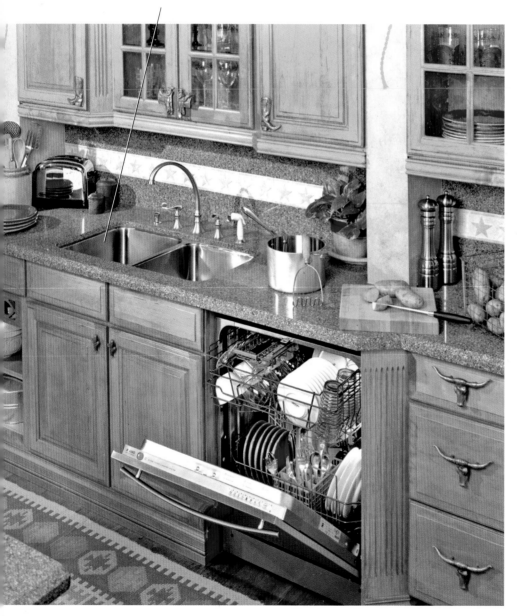

With the dishwasher next to the sink, there's plenty of room on both sides for the clean-up crew. Look through the glass cabinet doors—you can see that even the arrangement of the dishes has been well planned.

By putting special, hand-wash-only glasses above the sink and the more commonly used, dishwasher-safe dishes and glasses to the side of the dishwasher, the homeowner created an efficient traffic pattern for putting away the dishes.

This dishwasher is positioned to eliminate bending. If you or a family member has difficulty bending down, raise the dishwasher 9 to 12" off the floor. It will be easier to load and unload the dishes, and you'll have a raised counter, which adds an interesting design element and may be more comfortable for some users.

Undermount sinks don't have edges to collect grime or allow water to seep into cabinets like self-rimmed sinks. If you want an undermount sink, you'll need tile, solid-surface, or stone countertops.

This slide-out drawer conceals two trash cans behind a matching drawer front. Drawers of this sort have to support a fair amount of weight, so sturdy, high-quality glides and frames are a must.

When it comes to garbage/recycling areas, size matters. You need enough space for containers capable of holding several days' worth of trash and recycling. As any parent—especially parents of teenagers—will tell you, it's irritating to have food wrappers fall out on your feet when you open the door to the trash area. So, create space for large bins and a place to store trash bags and other supplies. If everything's within reach, maybe someone else will take out the trash for a change.

The sink is the most frequently used piece of equipment in a kitchen, and its size and placement are important. A standard sink is 6 to 8" deep, but the trend now is toward 10- to 12"-deep models. Combined with high-neck faucets, deep sinks are great for handling big pots and lots of dishes, and they make it easier to keep the water in the sink rather than all over the counters and the floors.

Deep sinks are not always the best choice, though. Taller people may find it uncomfortable to bend over a deep sink; raising the countertop a few inches may make it easier and more comfortable for them. On the other hand, shorter or seated users appreciate lower countertops and shallower sinks. Plan ahead for this—minor adaptations make a major difference.

A colored solid-surface countertop can be joined to a more traditional white sink, as in this Arts and Crafts kitchen. There are no seams or ridges either. The man-made composites of solid-surface materials can be fabricated in an almost infinite variety of shapes and sizes. Computerized cutting systems allow fabricators to create intricate, custom sink designs with ease.

Solid-surface sinks are second only to stainless steel when it comes to consumer choices for upscale kitchens. Why? Simple—they're quiet, easy to clean, and stain- and scratch-resistant. Any stains or scratches that do occur can be buffed or sanded out.

Installing a solid surface sink isn't a do-it-yourself project—they have to be fabricated and installed by trained and licensed craftspeople.

With this unique storage feature, these homeowners accomplished two important tasks: adding display storage and opening the room to the stairs. A project like this takes nothing but a few boards, a little trim, and a free afternoon.

Stainless steel sinks are always appropriate, especially combined with stainless appliances. Even with the number of shapes now available, traditional sinks like this one— rectangular with rounded corners—remain the most popular. Experts say rectangular sinks hold more, and rounded corners are easier to clean than square ones.

When it comes to economy and serviceability, you can't beat self-rimmed, stainless steel sinks. Typically, the least expensive and easiest to install of all sink styles, they never seem to go out of style. To ensure durability, 20 gauge steel is good, 18 is better—remember, the lower the number, the thicker the steel. The best sinks contain 18 percent chromium and have an undercoating on the bottom and sides of the basins to make them less noisy.

Stainless steel sinks are available with either satin or mirror finishes. Satin finishes are easy to maintain because minor scratches can be buffed out with a scouring pad. Mirror finishes scratch easily, so save them for sinks that are used gently, such as in a bar or butler's pantry.

Undivided, apron-front, farm-style sinks are everywhere these days, especially in model homes and design magazines. People who cook or entertain a lot like them because they can hold several large pots and pans with room to spare. These sinks are great for the right type of cook, but they're also quite expensive. Make sure it truly fits your cooking and living style before you invest in any sink—if you're like most people, you'll use it more than any other fixture in your kitchen.

Kitchen sinks can be categorized according to how they are mounted in the countertop.

• **Self-rimmed sinks** have rolled edges that rest directly on the countertop. This is the most common style because it's the easiest to install and typically the least expensive. The drawback is that the joint between the sink and countertop attracts dirt and has to be cleaned regularly.

• **Flush-mounted sinks** are recessed into the counter to sit flush with the surface. They blend nicely with countertops and are easy to keep clean.

• **Undermount sinks** fit below the countertop. They're often used with solid-surface, tile, or stone countertops, They can't be used with laminate countertops because the edges aren't waterproof from the top and from the sides.

• **Integral sinks** are molded basins that are actually part of the countertops. Stainless steel and solid-surface countertops often include integral sinks, which are attractive, virtually seamless, and very expensive. Minor damage can usually be buffed out of these materials, but major damage means the whole unit has to be replaced, an expensive proposition.

Enameled cast-iron sinks are attractive, extremely durable, and economical. A near automatic choice at one time, current trends have diminished their popularity. They're still excellent sinks, however.

Although others are available, self-rimming styles are common. Many homeowners searching for reasonably priced sinks find themselves considering both enameled cast-iron and stainless steel. Enamel sinks are available in many colors and shapes, which is a factor for many people. On the other hand, good quality models typically are more expensive than stainless steel, and the thickness of the material leaves the interior of an enamel sink slightly smaller than a stainless sink with the same dimensions. In some styles, the weight of the cast-iron may require special supports.

Today's enamel sinks don't chip easily, but they do have limits, and dropping heavy items in them may cause damage. Small chips can be repaired with a material sold at many hardware stores and home centers, but the repaired area will never look exactly the same.

Stain-resistant surfaces make routine maintenance simple; avoid abrasive cleaners.

Although self-rimmed styles are more typical, enameled cast-iron sinks are available in trendy styles and colors like this red, apron-front model.

*Idea*Wise

If you like islands but your kitchen doesn't have room for a permanent version, make one you can use when preparing meals and tuck back against a wall when it's not needed.

Start with a vintage table. Use a jigsaw to trim the tabletop flush with the aprons. Cut a top and two drop leaves from MDF (medium-density fiberboard) or solid-core veneer plywood. Sand the pieces, then paint or finish all four sides of each as desired.

Drill pilot holes and screw down through the new top into the old. Fill the holes with wood putty and touch up the finish.

Install drop leaf hinges (available at any

woodworker's store) to support the leaves. Attach a caster to each leg, and you're ready to roll!

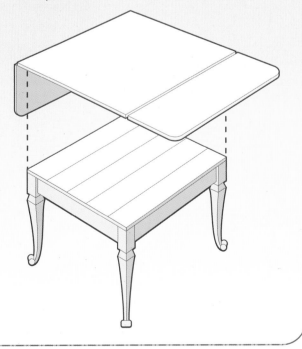

Cooking Centers

Do you or does someone in your family love to cook, or is cooking just a necessary task? Either way, having a well-planned cooking center makes meal preparation easier and more fun, or at least less of a hassle.

Decisions about cooktop and wall ovens or ranges depend on your cooking style and the available space. No matter what appliances you choose, remember that cooking centers revolve around the cooktop. Landing space—the area to either side of the cooktop—should be at least 9" on one side and 15" on the other. If the microwave is part of the cooking center, allow an additional 15".

With the cooktop in one island and the sink in another there's plenty of room for two or more cooks in a relatively modest space. Although a raised shelf was placed behind the sink so it can't be seen from the adjoining room, the cooking center's countertop was left open to maximize its workspace.

In a kitchen where an island serves as landing space for the wall oven, there should be no more than 48" between the front edge of the counter and the front of the oven.

In addition to the efficient use of space, this kitchen is remarkable for its storage capacity and dramatic color scheme. The back side of the cooking center island is lined with open shelves that house a cookbook library. The armoire holds everything from Grandmother's china to a prized collection of pitchers. Even the window seat gets into the act with apothecary-style drawers on each end and storage drawers under the seat.

The cranberry painted walls and oak cabinets mirror the colors of the painted oak islands and limestone countertops. The armoire sports a distressed finish in colors that coordinate with the cabinetry without matching. This combinations strike a pleasing balance between deep and neutral colors. After all, too much of a good thing is… just too much.

It's one of those "chicken or the egg" questions. Appliances first? Or cabinets? In truth, those decisions need to be made at about the same time. You can't order cabinets without knowing the dimensions of the appliances, but you're not ready to finalize the appliances until you've selected the cabinets.

Why? Because you may want to order matching cabinet fronts for the refrigerator and dishwasher. And even if you don't, the finish on the cabinets should play a part in deciding the color of the appliances. For example, white appliances mixed with dark cabinets or black glass appliances set into light cabinets create color blocks within the room. That may not be a problem in large kitchens and may even be a good idea in very contemporary designs, but it could be distracting in smaller or more traditional-style kitchens. Stainless steel appliances are favorite choices, at least partly because their soft glow blends into almost every color scheme.

When it comes to appliances, color is more than a matter of taste. Oven windows with black mesh usually offer the clearest view; the white screens or grids in all-white models can make it harder to see what's cooking.

Picture perfect efficiency.

Although there's certainly room for others, this elegant kitchen is efficiently arranged for one cook. Command central is directly in the center of the room: The large cooktop, surrounded by plenty of prep space, stands opposite the sink, which rests in the center of the island. The casual dining space on the far side of the island is easy to reach when it comes time to serve everyday meals. During parties, that space is a perfect place for guests to lounge while preparations are under way—close enough for conversation, but not underfoot.

When the task lighting doubles as accent lighting for dining, make sure the switches have dimmers. That way, you can cook under bright lights, dim the lights for the meal, then return them to full power while you clean up.

*Cooking pasta for a
crowd is a lot more
convenient when you
have a pot-filling
faucet near the cooktop.*

Vent hoods exhaust heat, moisture, grease, and cooking vapors from the air in your kitchen, protecting your cabinets and decorative surfaces—and your health. Normally, vents are installed with a ducting system that carries kitchen air to the outdoors. Local building codes may have specific ventilation requirements, so check with your building inspector or an HVAC contractor before buying a ventilation unit.

A true reflection of good taste, this cooking center features a stainless steel cooktop, gleaming metal vent hood and gorgeous metal tiles. Vent hoods are mounted above cooktops to catch rising heat, moisture, and grease. Vent hoods are either ducted or ductless. The ducted version uses a metal duct to vent air to the outdoors; a ductless vent simply recirculates air through filters. Ducted vent hoods are far more effective than ductless models. In fact, in many communities, ductless vents aren't allowed.

The National Kitchen and Bath Association recommends that every kitchen have a vent fan vented to the outside, and that the fan be capable of removing a minimum of 150 cubic feet of air per minute. Vent hoods are more important than you might think—one industry report indicates that inadequate ventilation can spread six quarts—*six quarts*—of grease throughout your home each year.

Vent hoods may be serious business, but they're also design opportunities.

Artistic panels make the vent hood the focal point of this kitchen. Any vent hood's primary reason for being is to provide ventilation, but here, as in many kitchens, it's also called upon to provide task lighting for the cooktop. The interior light fixtures are positioned to wash the backsplash, creating pleasant lighting for cooking.

The island and the large cabinets flanking the range are designed to create the impression of individual pieces of furniture.

In this compact kitchen, space is at a premium, but ventilation is still necessary. A vent hood/microwave unit provides both functions in one efficient, space-saving unit.

Going in an altogether different direction, the vent hood above this cooktop is concealed behind matching cabinet doors.

The downdraft system built into this stainless steel range makes a separate ventilation unit unnecessary, leaving space above the unit for cabinets.

Downdraft vents have blower units that vent through the back or bottom of a base cabinet. They are often used with modular ranges or cooktops, especially when they're installed in an island. Because a downdraft vent needs to work against the natural upward flow of heated air, it needs a more powerful motor than a standard vent hood.

Commercial-style cooktops are, by definition, rather large, and so are the vent hoods they require. Their sheer size offers design opportunities galore. These homeowners answered the challenge with a custom-built, tiled vent hood and backsplash combination.

Wow! When it comes to cooking units, the number of choices can make your head spin. Step into a home center or appliance store and you'll see a dizzying array of types, styles, sizes, and price ranges of products.

Choosing cooking units starts with deciding between gas and electric power. If you're working with existing space, it's usually far less expensive to use the same power source you currently have. If you're building or doing a major remodeling project, all options are open.

Remember that even gas units require a 120-volt, 20-amp outlet to provide power for the oven timers and flame-ignition modules.

If you like electric cooking, a smooth-top cooktop and a wall oven make an excellent combination. This island has loads of prep space on each side (the National Kitchen and Bath Association suggests at least 18" on one side) and storage all around. Here, the large center drawer holds plenty of pots and pans, and the smaller drawers are home to everything from spices to spatulas, hand towels to hot pads.

Smooth-top cooktops heat up in a flash, and they're easy to keep clean—fine characteristics for cooks-on-the-go. There is a price, though. Actually, there are several: Smooth tops typically are more expensive to purchase than coil burner cooktops, and they're more expensive to repair and replace. Plus, some models require flat-bottom cookware, which is another expense unless you already own it. Still, for many cooks, this popular combination is worth the expense.

The broad categories of cooking units are: range, cooktop, and wall oven. A *range* combines an oven and cooktop surface in one unit, a good choice when money or space is tight. A *cooktop* essentially is the burner portion of a range, with no oven. When you choose a cooktop, by default you'll also be choosing a separate oven or ovens.

• **Free-standing ranges** fit between cabinets or at the end of a row of cabinets.

• **Drop-in ranges** are unfinished on both sides and rest on a cabinet base.

• **Slide-in ranges** are unfinished on both sides and just slide into place between base cabinets.

• **Commercial-style ranges** are large, highly powered units that include four, six, or eight burners and an assortment of grills and griddles; they typically include several oven compartments as well. Burner output usually is 15,000 BTUs, much more than the 7,000 BTUs of standard burners. Commercial-style ranges are specially insulated, so they can be butted against walls or cabinets, and require heavy-duty vent hoods.

• **Commercial ranges** are generally not suited to home use, since they are not insulated well enough to meet code requirements and require complex, commercial-size ventilation units.

• **Drop-in cooktops** are installed in a hole cut in the countertop. Gas or electric, they include a variety of burners, some with interchangeable grills, griddles, and burners. Their controls are found on the top of the unit.

• **Commercial-style cooktops** overlap the cabinet case, so the controls are at the front of the unit. These cooktops include the same sort of variety of multiple burners, grills, and griddles as commercial-style ranges.

• **Single wall ovens** can be placed under drop-in cooktops or in full-height cabinets.

• **Double wall ovens** are placed in cabinets. Both single and double wall ovens are available in radiant, convection, microwave, or dual-duty products.

Plan a cooking center that fits your life.

When you're planning the kitchen, don't forget the microwave! It's so handy if you have children, and even gourmet cooks want a quick snack now and then. Although you can buy a microwave in every home center and discount store in North America, its selection and placement deserves the same careful thought as any other major appliance.

When built into the cabinets above a range, a microwave is positioned for adult use. That's fine if your family includes only adults, but not convenient if you have younger children who help with meal preparation or make their own snacks. (Standing on a chair to reach over the range or cooktop is not a good idea.)

Experts recommend that microwaves be placed so the bottom is 24 to 48" above the floor. However, 30 to 48" is the preferred range for average adult users, and 28 to 34" is typical for families that include children or smaller users.

Glass cabinet doors brighten a room, but clear glass lets everyone see exactly how organized you are. Obscured glass reflects light without giving away all your secrets.

An easy-to-clean range, built-in microwave, and plenty of prep space make this cooking center a joy to use. Landing space on either side of the range and refrigerator simplify meal preparation, especially when there's more than one cook in the kitchen.

If you have butcher block countertops, keep a cutting board handy. Cutting on the countertop could damage and stain it.

No detail was spared in planning this rustic kitchen. With an oversized gas range and a dramatic vent hood, the cooking center had an excellent foundation. A metal tile backsplash was added to preserve and protect the beautiful pine walls behind the range. The freestanding island is a convenient spot for food preparation, and the deep sinks handle large pots and pans with ease.

CHAPTER 4

Dining & Hospitality

W hen it comes to kitchen design, trends don't just come and go. They come and go, and come and go again. Eat-in kitchens have been in and out of fashion in several cycles since Colonial days, and kitchens have grown and shrunk correspondingly.

During the latest cycle, begun in the 1950s, eating and entertaining moved back into the kitchen, and kitchen designs expanded once again. In fact, virtually every home built in the last forty years provides at least some accommodations for eating in the kitchen; most homes built in the last ten years positively celebrate the idea.

If you're like most people today, you want to be able to eat and entertain in your kitchen. Once you've established that, the question becomes, "In what fashion?"

Is a harvest table too much? Peninsula or island space too little? Where will guests gather? These are questions that only you can answer, based on your family's style of living. As you look through the following pages, keep an eye out for designs and ideas that suit your family's patterns of cooking, eating, and entertaining.

A family who loves to entertain needs a kitchen that "works and plays well with others." In other words, a kitchen that meets the family's everyday needs, but is also arranged well for entertaining.

With its wide traffic aisles, this spacious kitchen is always ready for a party. The island, framed by a raised dining surface, hosts both the cooktop and sink. Although the cook can talk with family members or guests while working, the raised counter nudges others to the opposite side of the island, conveniently out of the work triangle.

Favorite wines are stored in easy proximity to the bar area.

Barware sparkles from inside a lighted accent cabinet hanging directly above a bar-style sink.

Accent lighting, such as these pendants, is switched separately and controlled with dimmers.

Double ovens offer plenty of capacity when it's time to bake family favorites or party delicacies.

What could be nicer than dinner in front of the fire on a cold winter evening? And with today's clean-burning, instant-on gas fireplaces, it's so easy and convenient.

In a kitchen with painted cabinets and a stained island, mixing a painted table and stained chairs is a nice touch.

In this Arts and Crafts inspired kitchen, a banquette nestles
below a bank of windows. It's a lovely spot for meals, and with the table
pulled aside, comfortable seating for parties. Another advantage of a banquette:
storage. Oodles of easy-to-reach storage can be hidden beneath the seat cushions.

In not-so-big kitchens, ingenuity triumphs over limited square footage.

An extra-wide, cutting board–style pull out hides in the dark until meal time, then makes its entrance. A surface like this needs to be at least 24" long to accommodate a place setting, and 28 to 32" wide to serve two.

Drop leaves on each side of a peninsula rise to the occasion

for dinners or parties, then fold away neatly. The cabinet opens to the front,

leaving the sides free for the space-saving drop-leaf mechanisms.

Color gives large presence to small spaces.

The contrast between this vivid blue wall
and the white beadboard below sets the stage
for a charming vintage-style dining area. The simple
pendant light provides light without distracting your
eyes from the framed prints and table settings.

Glass shelves produce the illusion that these black accessories are floating against the apple-green walls, making this corner look much bigger than it is. A sheet of glass balanced between a wall cleat and a stub wall serves dinner for one.

D o l l a r W i s e

An heirloom butcher block like the one on page 98 is ideal, but you can build a countertop dining space even without an expensive antique. Start by building a countertop out of ¾" exterior-grade plywood, 4-mil. poly-ethylene sheeting, ½" cementboard, and hardwood edging or v-cap edge tile. Attach support blocking to the plywood with screws, and add unfinished furniture legs, which are available at home centers and woodworking stores.

Set tile with thin-set mortar and let it dry. Grout and polish the tile, and you've got your very own, custom-built, informal dining space.

One table. Many settings.

Finished to match the cabinets, this table appears to be built in, but that's just an illusion.

For everyday meals, the table is set perpendicular to the wall of cabinets.

For parties, the table is shifted to the center of the room, an arrangement that makes it easier for guests to circulate.

IdeaWise

To emphasize the appearance of a peninsula extending from an island, change the flooring beneath it. For example, in a hardwood kitchen, set ceramic or stone tile in a shape to echo the peninsula, large enough for the surrounding seating.

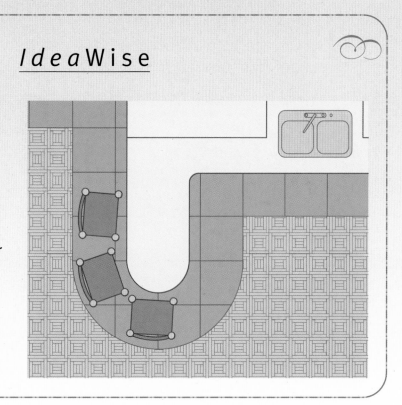

Although space was at a premium,

the homeowner wanted an island that could double as eating space. She also wanted to use an heirloom butcher block that had once belonged to her grandmother.

By adding legs to the butcher block and attaching a custom-tiled countertop to one side, she created a unique and meaningful work and dining space for the family.

Furniture-quality legs

and a center shelf support the butcher block beautifully.

Angled eating surfaces attached to the ends of the island take advantage of the available space in this long, narrow kitchen. The angles leave plenty of passage room around the island and add an interesting touch to the room.

*Design*Wise

Max Isley,
CKD, CBD, CMKBD

Hampton Kitchens
Wake Forest, NC

Plan dining and entertaining spaces to produce a comfortable flow for everyday dining as well as for parties. Think about where family members and guests will enter the kitchen and where they will stay once they're in the room.

• Create a snack or serving area within about 6 to 8' of the cooking area. Family members and guests will then be within comfortable distance of the cook without being underfoot.

• At a table or counter, provide at least 24" for each seated diner. If you wrap around the end of an island or table, allow a 36" return to comfortably accommodate two people at the corner.

• Think about clearance between seated diners and walls or furniture. A space of 24" is the minimum that allows you to avoid bumping the obstacle with the chair, but it takes at least 36" to be able to walk behind a seated guest.

• Don't automatically center a lighting fixture in an eating area. Decide what furniture you will use and where it will be, then position the lighting fixtures. Many times, it's best to set a fixture off center to leave room for furniture or artwork along the walls.

When the food preparation area and the dining area of a kitchen are open to one another but divided visually, neither should dominate.

A white brick wall anchors one side of this kitchen. To keep the food prep area from looking too heavy, the homeowners chose simple white cabinets, some with glass doors. Sunny yellow walls, framed by white cove molding, warm the whole room, and a glass-top table balances the whole equation.

The owners of this elegant kitchen wanted comfortable furnishings

that didn't compete with the stunning view. They established a delicate balance by selecting a
glass tabletop subtly supported by stone pillars and chairs with cream upholstery that melds with
the windows and trim. Then they added black-and-cream accents such as the floor covering and
fabrics repeated throughout the room. Simple but stunning.

Repeated materials unify open-plan rooms.

This island is big enough for quick snacks and casual meals for two.

A sun-filled space nearby holds a table and chairs, ready to host more formal meals or larger groups.

Taupe tumbled stone shows up on the broad expanse of backsplash and then again in a border set into the island's countertop. The iron and oak of the barstools and dining chairs echo the appliances and the cabinetry, and their taupe and white upholstery complements the stone tile.

A glossy, raised surface, supported by steel corbels,
rounds out the end of this island and provides plenty of dining space for
two without adding much to the footprint of the island.

CHAPTER 5

Lighting

Great kitchens have great lighting plans. Always. Take a look through this book, magazines, model homes, and the homes of your friends and family. Pretty soon, you'll see a pattern—the most attractive kitchens have excellent lighting. No matter how well equipped or how well laid out a kitchen is, it doesn't make the leap from good to great without efficient, attractive lighting.

Most people recognize that they need light in order to work comfortably in a kitchen. (Let's just say that no one wants to be using knives in the dark.) In response, many kitchens are built with most of the light concentrated in very bright central fixtures. But lighting the middle of the room and the ceiling isn't all that important. Getting light to the countertops, sink, and other prep and eating areas is.

The best way to light all those spaces is with individual sources. Recessed lights or track lights over a sink keep the area bright and shadowless even after the sun goes down. Pendants or spots over an island brighten valuable work and eating space. Strip lights on the underside of the cabinets reduce shadows. A pendant with a chrome-bottom bulb over the breakfast table provides soft light for the eating area.

You get the idea. The important thing is to come up with a plan that provides light for the many activities that take place in your kitchen and fits the style of the room. The photos throughout this chapter illustrate lots of ideas. Find your favorites and use them as starting points for creating a great lighting plan for your own kitchen.

If you're working with a kitchen designer, he or she is well prepared to make recommendations for lighting. If not, designers in home centers and salespeople at lighting stores are often very helpful. There are also professional lighting designers who, for a fee, will develop a lighting plan for you. You should have solid floor plans in hand before consulting with a lighting designer to take the best advantage of their expertise.

Words to the Wise

Ambient lighting sets the minimum level of lighting in a room, typically diffuse light from several sources. Windows, skylights, and overhead fixtures provide ambient light.

Task lighting provides brighter, functional light for individual work areas.

Accent lighting is subtle, indirect light that stresses points of decorative interest.

Recessed cans provide excellent general lighting. In insulated ceilings, make sure the cans are ventilated and the fixtures are rated for that purpose.

Under-cabinet lighting placed at the front edge of the cabinet reduces glare.

Lights concealed in cove moldings make ceilings look higher.

Light for dining areas should be controlled by dimmer switches.

In a well-lit kitchen, task, accent, and ambient light work together to create a comfortable environment for work and play.

Task lighting does just what its name implies—illuminates specific tasks. Task lighting should provide about three-fourths of the light in your kitchen. Accent lighting emphasizes details, such as art or favorite collectibles. Like spices in cooking, accent lighting is added to taste.

Light colors and shiny surfaces require less lighting than dark, matte surfaces. Lighting a kitchen like this, with dramatic contrast between cabinet units, presents special challenges. This flexible, adaptable track lighting allowed the homeowners to use a variety of fixtures and to position them effectively.

To reduce glare from shiny surfaces, use frosted fixtures or bulbs rather than clear ones.

When aimed at specific objects, track fixtures act as accent lights.

Don't be afraid to mix sizes and styles—even colors—of fixtures on one track. This track supports fixtures in two styles and several heights, delivering abundant light to individual task spaces.

Keep the bottom of pendants about 36" above the surface of an island,

or about 30" above a dining counter or table—higher if the ceiling is higher. To avoid painful (and potentially damaging) bumps in the night, hang the fixtures within the footprint of the island or counter.

Concealing lighting within display spaces gives favorite pieces the attention they deserve. Tiny puck lights are an easy, inexpensive way to light display spaces.

Daylight is the primary source of ambient light for most kitchens during the day. As a general rule, the area of a kitchen's windows should equal at least 10 percent of its floor area.

A gorgeous bank of windows provides plenty of daylight in this charming kitchen. Their unique shape, the white trim, and the absence of window treatments all emphasize their brightness within the deep colors of the wallcovering.

Light from corner windows bounces off adjacent walls, further brightening any room.

Place lights high on walls, washing the walls with light, to make rooms feel more spacious.

Skylights add wonderful, diffuse light. In this light-colored ceiling, light from the skylight is multiplied as it bounces off the rest of the ceiling and the walls. Skylights must be placed carefully. In hot climates, avoid south- or west-facing skylights or choose units that can be shaded in the afternoon.

Light from clerestory windows bounces off the ceiling and nearby walls, multiplying the ambient light they supply. In kitchens with high ceilings, placing windows above the cabinets doesn't sacrifice usable storage space and makes more sense than a standard soffit. And with uplights placed behind the framing for the upper cabinets, there's plenty of soft light from above, even when it's dark outside.

IdeaWise

Hide rope lights above a crown molding to create soft, comforting light to wash walls and ceilings. Install the crown molding 3 to 12" from the ceiling, using support blocks to hold it away from the wall. Cut a notch in the molding in an unobtrusive spot near a receptacle. Lay the rope lights in the trough between the wall and the molding. If you need more than one rope, remove the end caps and insert male/female connectors into the ends. Thread the cord down through the notch in the molding and plug it in. If you have the skills, you can hardwire low- or line-voltage rope lights into a nearby circuit.

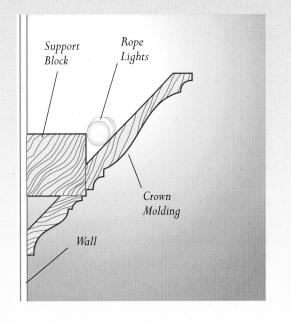

Support Block

Rope Lights

Crown Molding

Wall

The ceiling and beams are painted white to amplify and reflect light.

The beam supports track lighting for the island.

Each bank of windows is topped by track lighting, providing light in the evenings and on dreary days.

Under-cabinet fixtures light the countertop.

Window sashes separate the kitchen from the dining area without blocking light.

Glass doors let light pass through the cabinet uppers, highlighting the homeowners' collection of crystal.

Coordinating the lighting plan with the decorating scheme makes the most of both. This light, bright kitchen is the result of attention to details.

Contrast works miracles.
With white cabinets, appliances, and flooring, this kitchen could have looked cold and sterile. By using dark wallpaper and accessories, the homeowners provided contrast for the light to sparkle against. And look at that window in the backsplash area. Not large, but it's an eye catching feature that brings in just a little more light.

*Design*Wise

Connie Gustafson, CKD

Sawhill Custom Kitchens and Design, Inc.
Minneapolis, MN

Lighting is critical to the way your kitchen looks and to the way it works. Remember these suggestions:

• Place task light fixtures close enough to provide the proper amount of light for the tasks, and make sure the fixtures don't cast shadows on the work surface.

• Control ambient light with dimmer switches so you can adjust the light to create the effect you want.

• To add light inside cabinets with glass shelving and doors, use track or rope-type lighting at the front of the cabinet, along the sides. Add additional molding as necessary to hide the fixtures.

• If you use several pendants over an island, place them so each spread of light intersects with the light from the adjacent fixtures.

CHAPTER 6

Convenience & Communication

Folk wisdom is that the kitchen is the heart of a home. True, but in our busy world, it's also the nerve center, a place where communication, convenience, and comfort come together to serve and preserve a family's life.

Sometime during the 1970s and '80s, kitchen desks became almost standard equipment in new suburban homes. Despite their popularity, those desks weren't very practical—almost no one ever sat down at one for long, and the wasted space under them was a magnet for clutter. These days, kitchen desks have evolved into communications centers that include comfortable workspace, storage areas, message centers, and electronic equipment.

Electronics? Absolutely. In many kitchens, you'll find equipment that incorporates TV, music, and Internet access. Computers keep track of recipes, store grocery lists, and let you pay bills on-line. Some even have monitors that help you keep an eye on an infant napping in the nursery, teenagers hanging out in a basement recreation room, or visitors arriving at the front door.

All that equipment is great, but truly exceptional kitchens also make room for old-fashioned, face-to-face communication. A couple of cushy chairs. Maybe an ottoman or footstool. Good lighting. If you're really lucky, a fireplace.

In the next few pages, you'll see comfortable, attractive spaces where meals are created and served, work gets done, and people enjoy one another's company. Study them carefully for ideas you can incorporate into your own home.

Experienced kitchen designers report that most people considering a kitchen remodeling project want space that is, above all, versatile. Many potential remodelers dream of kitchens where they can supervise the kids' homework, pay bills, keep an eye on the evening news, and run a couple loads of laundry . . . all while dinner is cooking.

And, with careful planning, those dreams can become reality.

Set into a stunning wall of cabinets, this desk is flanked by bookshelves, file drawers, pigeonholes, and storage space. A true command center for the household.

The cherry trim coordinates with the desk surface, the door and drawer pulls, and the underlayer of the distressed finish.

A simple under-cabinet light illuminates the workspace.

Shelves hold a collection of cookbooks, reference manuals, and other family favorites.

Again, a desk space surrounded by drawers, cabinets, cubbyholes, and filing space pulls double duty in a kitchen. With the work surface cut at an angle, this desk takes maximum advantage of minimal space in this passageway to the kitchen.

Lights and glass doors transform otherwise wasted space into a dramatic display area.

Electrical receptacles and phone jacks are must haves for desk areas. Depending on your television preferences, Internet access, and computer systems, you may want to add cable jacks as well.

Framed by a cereal pantry and a cabinet filled with antique china, this window provides both light and an attractive view. In a clever use of space, the homeowners nestled a desk beneath the window and added a cookbook shelf below to discourage the clutter that sometimes collects under kitchen desks.

Elevating the food preparation area of this kitchen creates a sense of division without full walls. The long computer counter, flanked with drawers and filing cabinets, offers plenty of room to spread out books and papers for homework, household management, or Internet research and correspondence. Well-placed windows flood the area with light, making the small space feel spacious and open.

A well-designed corner nook shelters this home office. By angling the ceiling and adding a window, the homeowners created the sense of a distinct area within the room. Having a computer in the kitchen is surprisingly handy. It handles recipes, nutrition information, and grocery lists as well as the family finances and the children's homework.

Ingenuity wins again. With today's portable equipment and wireless Internet access, you can make efficient workspace even without the luxury of a permanent setup. A drop-leaf section on a cabinet base can be called into service or folded away, depending on the needs of the moment.

Some of us like it and some of us don't, but television is a daily fact of life for most families. Creating space for it just makes sense.

A television doesn't have to take center stage. Set into a bank of cabinets, a small set isn't intrusive. And if you add doors that slide out from the sides and then fold closed, it can blend into the room when no one's watching.

Surrounding cabinets and cubbies give you places to store the remote and DVDs or tapes. Installed in upper cabinets adjacent to an informal eating area, this small TV is present without overwhelming the area.

A large space like this calls for a large television.

If you have a large kitchen and want to be able to see the television from several angles, set a cabinet case on a swivel.

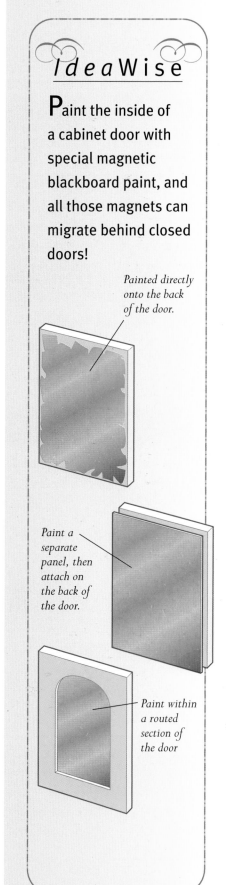

Sometimes communication can be as simple as a message board in a central location.

The wall in this dining area sports a large, framed black-board where the family keeps lists, leaves messages for one another, and makes miscellaneous notes.

A blackboard framed into the end of the cabinets acts as a message center in this compact kitchen.

Whether it's an adjacent family room or a small seating area, most homeowners find that the ultimate communication tool is room for the family to hang out in the kitchen and talk.

Not exactly a family room and far more than just a couple of chairs in the corner, a comfortable seating area brings this kitchen to life. It's a great place to lounge while meals are prepared and a wonderful place to wake up with coffee or unwind at the end of the day.

If you're lucky enough to have an area like this, furnish it with swivel chairs that can face the fireplace or the food preparation area, depending on the activity of the moment.

Kitchens that are open to adjacent rooms certainly encourage communication. This family room is set apart from the kitchen just a bit, but close enough for comfortable conversation.

*Design*Wise

Stephanie J. Witt, CKD, CBD, CMKBD

Kitchens by Stephanie, Ltd. Grand Rapids, MI

e find that most kitchen communications are brief, and the standard low desks are inefficient, awkward, and hard on the back. To avoid these issues:

• Raise the desk to 42" and incorporate a wide stack of drawers on both sides, including one or two lateral filing cabinet drawers.

• Place pigeonholes in the wall cabinets above the desk, and line the inside of the cabinet doors with cork. Install an electrical outlet and telephone line inside the cabinet to service a computer and portable phone.

• Enclose the area with tambour doors similar to those found on appliance garages. The doors may stay open most of the time, but everyone has days when they need to close doors over work in progress.

If you really want a seating area but don't think you have the room, look again with a more critical eye. You may have more options than you first realize.

When you adopt a less conventional attitude, even a chandelier in the middle of the room doesn't dictate that it be used as a dining area. You can remove the fixture and cover the electrical box with a blank plate painted to blend into the ceiling. Voilà! A seating area materializes before your eyes. With enough counter space and possibly a formal dining room, no one will ever miss another table.

The atrium area of this kitchen is furnished as a seating area rather than the more conventional dining space it might have been. The bank of windows and luxurious sofa are an irresistible combination the family appreciates every day.

Dream Bathrooms

Folk wisdom tells us that everything old is new again, an idea that is as true of bathrooms as anything else. Today's trend watchers report that the average family bath has doubled in size since the 1950s and that large, comfortable bathrooms including luxurious baths and showers are second only to gourmet kitchens on the list of upscale home buyers' requests.

This information is reported as news in industry magazines, regarded as a burgeoning trend, and catered to by manufacturers, building contractors, and designers. All the while, we collectively imagine that we are—at this moment in history—somehow unique in our interest in bathrooms.

And yet, in the Minoan Palace of Knossos on the isle of Crete, archeologists found what many believe was the first flushing "water closet," or toilet, circa 1700 B.C. Tiled bathrooms and self-draining tubs connected to underground piping have been discovered in the ruins of Olynthus, a city destroyed by Philip of Macedon in 432 B.C.

There's no doubt that elaborate baths and showers are popular today, but no more so than in ancient Rome, where public baths were the centers of entertainment and gossip. After all, the baths of Diocletian are said to have seated over 3,000 bathers.

Such marvels of plumbing were destroyed along with the ancient civilizations that built and enjoyed them. It took over 3,000 years for another flushing toilet to be devised by J. D. Harrington in 1596, and several hundred more years for modern plumbing to find its way to the general population.

Modern plumbing literally changed the world, reducing as it did the spread of typhus, cholera, and other bacteria-borne disease. A new, expanded, or redecorated bathroom probably won't change your world, but it certainly can radically improve your everyday experience of it. After all, an attractive, functional bathroom soothes, rejuvenates, revives, refreshes, and comforts us.

As the world outside our doors fill with stress and distress, we're investing more and more in our homes, trying to turn them into islands of peace and calm and rest.

Improving or adding a bathroom typically is a sound investment. In most regions of the country, about 90 percent of the money invested in a bathroom remodeling project is returned at the sale of the house—more if the project adds a master bathroom or a second bathroom to a one-bathroom home. Local real estate brokers and building contractors can give you more information on what you can expect in your region.

The National Kitchen and Bath Association, an organization of professional kitchen and bath planners, offers worksheets and self-surveys to help you assess your needs and wants, design guidelines, and connections to professionals in your area at their website nkba.com. The NKBA is an excellent source of both information and inspiration—a good place to start.

Accessibility Matters

Adults with no physical challenges of any sort are not the norm, they are the exception by far. In fact, according to some counts less than 25 percent of the adult population can claim such status. And yet, when accessibility is mentioned in regard to bathrooms, most people conjure up images of austere, clinical looking rooms filled with unattractive adaptive devices, utilitarian fixtures and not much style. That may have been true at some point, but it most definitely is not true today.

The issue of accessibility has evolved into concern for Universal Design—design that works for everyone. Universal Design addresses issues from slip-resistant flooring to adequate lighting, from grab bars and curbless showers to counter height—issues of concern for every body, every age, every size. Addressing these issues adds to everyone's enjoyment of a bathroom and it by no means detracts from its design or style. Today's cabinets, fixtures, and fittings are as attractive as they are functional.

As you choose your bathroom fixtures and materials, consider improving the safety and accessibility of your bathroom as part of your project. Many products that enhance safety and accessibility can easily be installed in less than an hour. During a major renovation project, integrating these features is even easier. When considering safety and ease of use, you'll need to include nearly all aspects of the bathroom: flooring, fixtures, cabinets, showers and tubs, electrical systems, and doors.

How to Use This Section

The following pages are packed with images of interesting, attractive, and efficient bathrooms. And although we hope you enjoy looking at them, they're more than pretty pictures: they're inspiration accompanied by descriptions, facts, and details meant to help you plan your bathroom project wisely.

Some of the rooms you see here will suit your sense of style, while others may not appeal to you at all. If you're serious about remodeling or building a new bathroom, read every page—there's as much to learn in what you don't like as in what you do. Look at each photograph carefully and take notes. The details you gather are the seeds from which areas for your new bathroom will sprout.

CHAPTER 1

Walls, Floors & Ceilings

The walls, floor, and ceiling define a room: its size, shape, appearance, and—most of all—the ways it's used. That's right: the ways it's used. Surface treatments divide bathrooms into wet and dry zones, areas that can and cannot withstand constant exposure to water.

Like beauty, walls, floors, and ceilings are more than just skin deep. For example, although the surface tile virtually defines an area as a wet zone, the underlying wall material itself must stand up to moisture. No matter what the surface treatment, cementboard should be used in wet zones rather than drywall.

Some bathroom floors have to be built to carry a serious load. Think about it: a gallon of water weighs about 8.34 pounds, and a two-person tub can hold up to 120 gallons of water. That's about 1000 pounds of dead weight, even before you and your sweetie settle in for a long soak. No wonder the floors beneath large tubs and whirlpools require additional structural support.

In this chapter, you'll see walls, floors, and ceilings in many shapes, sizes, and finishes. Take a look at everything. The most obvious choice isn't always the best option.

Subtle variations in textures and colors on the walls, floors, and ceiling create an interesting, dynamic room. Here, white, blues, and grays create a tranquil foundation for this bath; detailed molding and trim define the space throughout the room; and the mixed surface coverings—granite on the countertops, glass tile on the floor, and ceramic subway tile on the walls—add interest.

Strategically placed wall sconces allow light to be shared throughout the space.

White molding helps to define the space and draw the eye up toward the beautiful, spacious ceiling.

Simple, open glass shelving allows light from the windows to filter through the entire room while also taking advantage of valuable vertical storage space.

If you choose the clean look of an all-white bath, consider grounding the room with a darker floor covering like the glass mosaic tile shown here.

Walls

Never given much thought to the bathroom walls? You're not alone. Other than old jokes about the writing on them, bathroom walls don't get much attention. However, the walls typically present the largest surface in a bathroom and anyone who ignores them misses a wealth of design opportunities.

Words to the Wise

Cementboard: A substrate used under ceramic tile and stone. Cementboard remains stable even when exposed to moisture, a critical issue in bathrooms.

Fiber/cementboard: A thin, high-density underlayment used in wet areas where floor height is a concern.

Greenboard: Drywall treated to withstand occasional moisture. It's a good choice for bathroom walls outside wet zones.

Drywall: Panels consisting of a gypsum core covered in paper.

Painted drywall is a perennial favorite because paint is inexpensive, attractive and oh-so-easy to change. If you use the right type of paint and apply it properly to the right drywall material, the walls will look great for as long you want to live with the color. And—perhaps best of all—a gallon or two of paint and a free afternoon is all it takes to give the room a facelift when color trends or your tastes change.

Be sure walls in wet zones start with cementboard; greenboard is appropriate for walls outside the wet zones. (See *Words to the* Wise.)

Look for specially-formulated paint with an additive that helps prevent the growth of mold and mildew. (Even so, it's vital to provide ventilation. Run a vent fan when bathing or showering and open the windows when possible.)

Trompe l'oile ("fool the eye") painting techniques create fantasy worlds in bathrooms. The acrylic paints typically used for trompe l'oile are durable enough for bathrooms, even heavily used family baths.

Here, the painter presents a koi's-eye view of a water garden. The theme is continued in the stained-glass treatment of the window, the decorative sink, and the mosaic tile countertop. Subtle touches such as these water-colored towels and soap reinforce a dramatic theme without reaching the level of overkill, which is especially important in a small room.

Medicine cabinets can be nestled between wall studs quite easily in non-load-bearing walls. It's possible to do this in load-bearing walls as well, but generally requires that support be added to transfer the load to the surrounding framing.

Wallpaper dresses a wall like nothing else, and—after a decade-long absence—it's returning to the forefront of the decorating scene. With reasonably priced laser levels available everywhere, it's easier than ever to get it straight.

Wallpaper labeled "scrubbable" is made to withstand exposure to moisture, which is especially important in a family or often-used bathroom. Still, humidity has to be controlled in bathrooms that include wallpaper: Install an efficient vent fan and use it while showering or bathing.

Used in bathing rooms for centuries, ceramic tile is still the number one material chosen for today's bathrooms, probably because it's so versatile. Tile can be smooth or rough, intricate or simple, colorful or muted. It provides excellent insulation, resists fading in any light, repels moisture, and doesn't give off toxic fumes in a fire. And it's so easy to clean that tile rated as "impervious" is often used in operating rooms and commercial kitchens, where cleanliness can be a matter of life and death.

Wall tile is thinner than floor tile and sometimes has a finer finish. You can use floor tile on walls but it's thicker and heavier, which can make it difficult to set. Also, fewer styles of trim are available for floor tile, which may make it harder to finish off all the edges.

Wall layouts are sometimes elaborate and tend to have lots of exposed edges, so manufacturers offer a variety of trim and border pieces for wall tile.

Most wall tile is self-spacing, which means the individual tiles have small flanges on each edge to help maintain even spacing.

Sophisticated techniques allow tile manufacturers to produce tile that imitates natural stone, metal, and other materials, often at lower prices.

The combination of subtle color and glazing give this porcelain tile the look of polished stone.

Imagination and innovative materials take bathroom walls to extraordinary heights.

These wall panels aren't tile or stone, but concrete. That's right: concrete. Today, concrete is being used in a surprising number of places—anywhere one might put tile, laminate, solid surface, or natural stone.

Wall panels like these—as well as the tub surround—are cast, then hand polished and sealed to make them stain and water resistant. Concrete is a fabulous material, adored by those willing to accept its eccentricities. Devotees consider the variations in color and texture and the characteristic hairline cracks a part of its appeal.

If you're considering concrete in your bathroom, talk with your designer or supplier first, and make sure you understand the nature of concrete and the care it requires.

Sealer and paste or beeswax help concrete panels repel water and stains. The finish requires maintenance every three months or so.

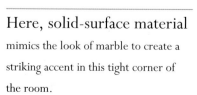

Here, solid-surface material mimics the look of marble to create a striking accent in this tight corner of the room.

Smooth river rock set in mortar adds **texture** to this contemporary bath, proving that stone doesn't need to be cut or polished to be attractive. Filled with irregular shapes, the rock wall is balanced by the smooth lines of the rest of the room. Other elements in the room should support rather than compete with dominant features, such as this wall.

(above) White tile and fixtures sparkle against the mellow tones of tongue-and-groove wood in this spa-like bathroom. Wood brings warmth and richness to any room, but careful thought and preparation is required to keep wood beautiful in a bathroom.

Some wood—such as teak, bamboo, and cedar—is naturally water resistant and, with the application of special sealers, can safely be used on walls as well as floors and even countertops.

Long a favorite in bathrooms, painted beadboard walls lend a traditional air to modern bathrooms. Paint seals the wood, protecting it against moisture and stains. Semi-gloss or gloss paint, sometimes referred to as "enamel," provides the best protection.

Floors

Bathroom floors have a pretty tough assignment: they need to stand up to drips, drops, and splashes of water, remain safe and comfortable in any situation, and look good while performing these remarkable feats.

Let's talk safety first. More than 25 percent of all household accidents happen in the bathroom. Falls while getting in or out of the tub are the most common household accident, a fact that points out how important it is to choose slip-resistant flooring.

If you're considering tile or stone, check the labeling for something called a "Friction Coefficient," which rates slip resistance. Floor tile must have a friction coefficient of at least .6 to meet standards set by the Americans with Disabilities Act, a good guideline to follow. If the floor covering you're considering isn't labeled this way, ask your designer, contractor, or retailer for more information on slip resistance.

Some floor coverings are undeniably appealing but can't tolerate exposure to water. These floor coverings simply don't belong in bathrooms, where water is the name of the game. Unless bathroom flooring is water resistant or well sealed, problems will develop. Talk with your designer, contractor, or retailer to make sure the floor covering and/or finishes you choose are appropriate.

And, finally, we come to appearance. With the range of reasonably priced materials available, there's no reason to settle for anything less than a floor you love. Keep shopping until you find the colors, textures, and designs that fit your taste and lifestyle.

Horizontal lines in the design visually expand small spaces.

Subtle colors in striking combinations produce a dramatic floor for this luxurious bath. Although the stone is set in a fairly simple pattern, the color combination gives it zing. Stone extends up the walls as well, seamlessly integrating the floor and walls to make the room appear larger than it actually is.

Smooth stone, especially marble, can be cold to the touch. If you love the look of stone but hate to step from a warm shower onto an icy floor, consider a radiant heating system. Radiant floor heat consists of a network of wires or water lines running between the subfloor and the floor covering that keeps even stone floors toasty.

The grandeur look of marble is unmatched by any other floor covering. Being that it is so luxurious it does require special pampering (see page 153).

(below) Vinyl flooring in a faux-crocodile pattern gives this contemporary bathroom exotic flair.

Light colors and simple lines contrast beautifully with dark, dramatic floors.

The faux-crocodile texture provides excellent slip resistance.

Flooring Options

Each type of flooring has unique characteristics and installation techniques. Appearance is important, but so are safety, durability, ease-of-care, and environmental impact.

VINYL

Inexpensive, easy to clean, and durable, vinyl flooring is available in a huge variety of colors, patterns, and styles.

Sheet vinyl with felt backing is glued to the subfloor.

Sheet vinyl with PVC backing is glued only along the edges, called a perimeter bond.

Vinyl tiles, which typically come in 12 or 16" squares, generally are not the best choice for bathrooms because the seams leave the subfloor vulnerable to water damage.

CERAMIC TILE

Ceramic tile is made from clay pressed into shape and then fired in a kiln. Glazed ceramic or porcelain tile produces superior bathroom floors—durable, water resistant, and colorful. Porous and softer than glazed tile, unglazed tile is rarely an ideal choice for a bathroom. If used, it must be well sealed and carefully maintained.

Ceramic tile is set in thin-set mortar and then grouted. It's a step-by-step process that requires time and careful planning.

NATURAL STONE

Granite, marble, slate, limestone, and travertine are available in slab and tile form. Stone requires careful upkeep when used in bathrooms, particularly marble. The most easily stained of the natural stones, marble has to be sealed with penetrating sealer and maintained regularly.

HARDWOOD

Hardwood floors look and feel warm; they're also durable and easy to clean. Properly sealed and maintained they can be used in bathrooms, but be aware of the upkeep and precautions required before choosing hardwood for a bathroom.

BAMBOO

Bamboo flooring is durable, attractive, and environmentally sound. Bamboo is a sustainable resource because it regenerates in three to five years. Like wood, it can be used in bathrooms if properly prepared and maintained.

LINOLEUM

Linoleum is an all-organic laminate, a layer made from linseed oil, wood flour, and pine resins bonded to a jute backing. It's kind to the environment, allergy sufferers and chemically sensitive people.

CONCRETE

Polished concrete is available with any number of decorative finishes from matte to super glossy— even an acid-etched surface that can look like stone or marble. Depending on the finish, it may require a fair amount of maintenance. Some manufacturers recommend waxing their concrete products monthly and stripping and resealing it quarterly. Shop around for a product and finish that meet your needs. Also, keep in mind that concrete develops hairline cracks, one of its charms for enthusiasts, but a characteristic that may not be loved by everyone.

Another concern with concrete: weight. Any floor may require additional support, and in the upper stories of wood-framed homes, concrete floors simply may not be practical. Check with a contractor or building inspector for support requirements before investing in concrete floors.

Sometimes you want the floor to be the star of the show; sometimes you don't. Here, a simple cream square tile floor lets the tile-clad walls handle the spotlight.

Glazed tile doesn't need to be sealed, but grout does. After it has fully cured (check manufacturer's directions), apply grout sealer to the grout lines only. Using a small sponge brush or special wheel-like applicator makes it much easier to keep the sealer where you want it.

When you want the floor to recede, choose grout that blends rather than contrasts with the tile. Less contrast helps the tile meld into the room; more contrast makes it pop.

Profiled backsplash tiles match the floor and tub surround.

Three different rectangular tiles create an intriguing border for this tub surround.

Edge tile have to be individually cut to complete a diagonal set.

Tile collections create eye-popping designs.

These collections often include different sizes, shapes, and finishes of the same tile—sometimes even different tones of the same color. Here, tile in various shapes and finishes are combined to dramatic effect. Highly polished tiles cover the walls, while matte finished versions of the same tile make up the floor.

Diagonal sets require some extra cutting for the edge tile and setting one section of tile on the diagonal within a straight set requires a second set of reference lines. However, once the lines are drawn, diagonal sets are no more difficult than straight.

Tile extends from the vanity area to the bathing area in this master suite. A woven pattern is maintained throughout, but blue accents give way to solid color in the next room. The result is a smooth transition from one space to the next.

If you have a large bathroom, there's no rule that the entire floor all needs to be identical. Create visual separation between areas with accents, borders, and other trim.

*Idea*Wise

Want an easy way to create a floor that makes a statement? Go mosaic. It's amazingly easy to create patterns—even elaborate designs—when you start with mosaic tile mounted to mesh backings. Reasonably priced prearranged borders are widely available at home centers and tile stores.

For extra pizzaz lay a prearranged border at the perimeter of the room, then connect the floors to the walls with a combination of baseboard tile, borders, and liners.

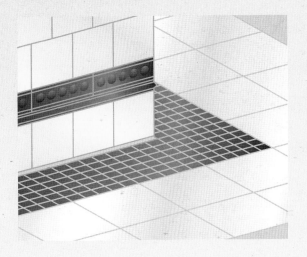

Light washes the walls, illuminating the tile as well as the room.

A spectacular, specially fabricated wood-and-glass sink floats against the wall.

The first floor tile and the top and bottom wall tile are cut to an equal size, which balances the layout.

A wooden mat occupies the floor in front of the sink, providing a slip-resistant surface in this wet zone.

Unique fixtures and accessories glow against the sleek flannel-gray floor and walls of this contemporary bathroom. A solid gray material might have been boring here, but the subtle color variations of this tile keep the background interesting.

Careful planning is vital to this look: Minimizing cut tile and grout lines helps the individual pieces of granite meld into a harmonious whole.

The natural colors of slate set a rich color scheme for this striking, somewhat masculine-looking bathroom. The wall covering, countertop, and even the sink vessel and toilet relate to the deep tones found in the slate.

Choose slate for a bathroom floor only if you understand and appreciate its properties. Because it's a relatively soft material, slate requires periodic maintenance and shows wear over time, especially scratches. Slate is a good choice for those who enjoy materials that reflect the passage of time, but may not be the ideal choice for someone who prefers materials that look new forever.

Cut tiles form baseboards, creating a smooth transition from floor to wall.

*Design*Wise

DeWitt Talmadge Beall

DeWitt Designer Kitchens
Studio City, CA

- Install heating mats under tile or stone to provide a warm and friendly surface for bare feet.

- Create a rug-like pattern in tile or stone by setting tile on the diagonal in the center of the room and framing the sides with tile on the square.

- Create a lit niche in the wall to display a beautiful object. Trim with distressed wood, stone, stucco, tile, or Venetian plaster.

- Trim the perimeter of skylights with crown molding that conceals xenon festoon lighting to create an after-dark romantic glow.

- Use "Meshed Stone" to cover walls for a unique texture. To "mesh stone," select a 12 × 12" stone tile, such as a marble, cut it into 1 × 1" squares, then mount the squares randomly on nylon mesh for easy installation.

- Install indirect or dimmable lighting that is easy on the eyes for bathers reclining or relaxing in the tub.

Two of the many faces of concrete are shown here. That's right: both the typical square floor tile shown at left and the custom pattern shown at right are concrete.

No longer drab or boring in the least, concrete can be colored with a huge variety of pigments, cast into virtually any shape imaginable, and given any finish from matte to glossy. A well-sealed concrete floor is both stain and water resistant, but it can be quite heavy. Concrete floors require careful maintenance and may require additional structural support. If you're considering concrete in your bathroom, talk with your designer or supplier first, and make sure you understand the structural support that's necessary as well as the nature of concrete and the care it requires.

Floor-warming Systems

Imagine stepping from a warm shower onto an equally comfortable floor. It can happen in any weather if you install a floor warming system beneath the floor covering in your bathroom.

Floor-warming systems are an affordable luxury. Systems that rely on warm water to heat the floor typically require professional installation; other systems employ electric resistance wires that heat up when energized, similar to an electric blanket, and can be installed by confident do-it-yourselfers. Either way, the system is installed beneath the floor covering and wired to a thermostat to control the temperature and a timer that can turn it on and off automatically.

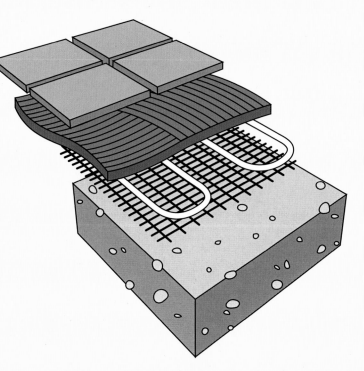

Medicine cabinets tucked into wall cavities provide the kind of storage that can be missing in bathrooms without vanity cabinets.

Painted quarter-round eases the transition between the floor and walls.

Wooden bases lift the pedestals into position to shield the plumbing from view and protect users from hot water supply pipes.

Protect wood floors with high-quality, water-resistant sealer.

Wood covers all the bases in this bathroom—floors, walls, and ceilings. To provide contrast, each surface is treated to a different finish. Stained planks warm the floor; painted car-siding boards embrace the walls; pickled tongue-and-groove paneling highlights the ceiling.

Wood brings beauty to a bathroom, but it also brings potential problems—chiefly water damage. Some woods, such as teak, redwood, and mahogany, are naturally water resistant, but other varieties tend to expand and contract as temperatures and humidity levels fluctuate, which can lead to warping.

To safely use wood in a bathroom, make sure every inch is protected with a high-quality, water-resistant sealer, conscientiously use the vent fan when showering or bathing, and wipe up spills and splashes quickly and thoroughly.

Ceilings

The ceilings in most bathrooms are constructed with a drywall base and covered with paint or wallcovering, a good alternative, but not the only one. No, the limit for bathrooms ceilings is only a little short of the sky itself. Ceilings can be covered in wood, tile, or metal; they can play host to decorative beams or even trompe l'oile murals. In short, any material that's attractive, moisture resistant, and able to be structurally supported can be used on a bathroom ceiling.

(left) Choose a ceiling material that supports the theme of the room. Here, tongue-and-groove paneling and timber beams complement the log-cabin ambience.

Wood requires protection anywhere in a bathroom, even a ceiling. Although it's unlikely that water will be splashed up onto the ceiling very often, warm, moist air will rise to the ceiling every time the tub or shower are used. A yearly coat of sealer keeps a wood ceiling beautiful and carefree.

(right) When circumstances call for moisture resistance, think ceramic tile. Other materials might fail here, but the ceramic tile ceiling, walls, and floor of this luxurious bathroom withstand even the copious amounts of moisture released by the steam room and large, sunken whirlpool tub.

Strong architecture requires subtle treatments.
Here, cream paint on flat-finished drywall encourages the interplay of shadows along the dramatic angles of the ceiling and walls.

Feel free to be a perfectionist when it comes to a flat finish on drywall ceilings—skillful craftsmanship and real attention to detail is required to make a ceiling like this look its best.

Wallpaper draws the ceiling down to the walls, creating a more intimate feeling in this airy bathroom.

Good ventilation is essential in wallpapered bathrooms—excessive moisture can loosen the adhesive and cause the seams and edges to peel up. Powder rooms, bathrooms with standard tubs rather than whirlpools or showers, and rooms with operable windows are good candidates for wallpapered ceilings or walls. A wallpapered bathroom, as any other, needs a ventilation fan rated to handle the square footage of the room, and family members need to use the fan when bathing or showering.

Skylights bring light and energy to a bathroom.

Many designers say that skylights are the best thing you can do for a ceiling. Most suggest units that can be opened and closed with remote controls, feature low-E glass, and have several modes of light control.

Take care when placing skylights: In hot climates, avoid south- or west-facing skylights or choose units that can be shaded in the afternoon.

In this light-colored ceiling, light from the opposing skylights is multiplied as it bounces between the skylights, window, ceiling, and walls.

In this windowless bathroom, skylights contribute lovely and much appreciated light. Be especially careful with the placement of inoperable skylights—north or east exposures and shaded areas are the best choices.

CHAPTER 2

Storage & Display

Remember the old saying that you can never be too rich or too thin? That opinion is—and always has been—debatable, but this much is true: Most of us can never have enough bathroom storage. It takes a whole lot of lotions and potions to maintain the youthful appearance to which so many of us aspire.

According to people who research these sorts of things, the average American woman applies 33 products to her face and body each morning before leaving the house. You read that right—*thirty-three* products. Add the products used by a spouse or partner and a child or two, and you're looking at 40 to 50 containers competing for space in the bathroom. And that's for an average family—high-maintenance folks have an even larger array.

And so we come to the subject of storage, which unleashes a series of questions. How many cabinets do you need, and should they be built-in or freestanding? Closed cabinets or open shelves? Is a pedestal sink workable or do you need a vanity?

Only you can answer these important questions, but we're here to help. We invite you to read through this chapter with an open mind. Take notes about what you find interesting and attractive, then spend some time thinking about your family's habits and routines. The best storage solutions are ones that meet your specific needs and suit your personal taste.

Cabinets

Whether you're adding or remodeling a bathroom, cabinetry is one of the most important investments you'll make. Some elements—floor coverings, paint and wall coverings, and so forth—change along with design trends. (Experts estimate that bathrooms are freshened, on average, every seven to ten years.) Cabinetry, however, has a very long useful life and is likely to remain in place for many years.

If you're in the process of a remodeling project and your cabinets work well, consider painting or refacing them. Paint is an option only for wood cabinets, but both wood and laminate cabinets can be refaced by installing new cabinet doors, drawer fronts, and matching veneer on face frames and cabinet ends.

Ready-to-assemble cabinets are available through home centers and furnishings retailers. Typically offered in set sizes, standard pieces are configured to fit the room.

Stock cabinets, available through home centers, are offered in a range of standard sizes, usually in 3" increments. A limited variety of door styles and colors can be purchased off the shelf or delivered within a few days.

Semi-custom cabinets are manufactured in hundreds of standard sizes, finishes, and styles. You can buy these cabinets through home centers, kitchen designers, and contractors. Following a plan that you or you and a designer have created, your cabinets are built to order according to the manufacturer's standard specifications.

Custom cabinets are built by a custom manufacturer or by a cabinet shop. In either case, you can expect high-quality materials and workmanship as well as luxurious details and accessories. You can also expect to pay a price for these luxuries.

Bathroom cabinets should meet your needs. Consider who uses the bathroom, how and when, and plan storage that works for your life. Here, a combination of doors, drawers, and open shelves store toiletries and grooming essentials for the two adults who use the room, typically one at a time.

More users often requires more sinks and mirrors, but more cabinets are not always necessary. This owner's suite includes plenty of room for both of the homeowners to get ready for the day without bumping into one another. The look is zen and simple. The floating countertop offers plenty of open space to maintain an uncluttered feel.

Words to the Wise

On framed cabinets, the exposed edges of the cases are covered with flat (face) frames. The doors may be set into the frames or overlay them; the hinges are attached to the frames and the doors. Framed cabinets require more materials but often are less exacting to build than frameless. They are preferable in historic or traditional-style homes.

On frameless cabinets, the exposed edges are covered with edge banding and the doors cover nearly the entire case. The door hinges are attached to the doors and the sides or ends of the cases. Frameless cabinets require less material but can be more time consuming to build than framed. The structure allows for wider doors and better accessibility.

Cabinets do not have to be ornate or even prominent to get the job done. The main goal for storage in a bathroom—or any other room, for that matter—is to keep things near their point of use. Simple. Hair dryers should be housed near mirrors; towels near the shower, tub, and sinks; bubble bath near the tub. You get the idea.

The trick to planning efficient storage is first to figure out what is used and where, then to decide how and where those things will be stored. Consider placing pull-out shelves and drawers, hampers, and trash cans behind closed doors. Don't underestimate the importance of well-placed towel bars and robe hooks. These small details play a large role in the convenience level of daily living.

Make-up mirrors are cleverly inlaid within these vanity mirrors, saving countertop and storage space.

The space between these sinks leaves plenty of counter space around both sinks. The NKBA recommends 36" from centerline to centerline of double sinks.

Bold and beautiful, the stain on this countertop creates an intimate feeling that might otherwise be missing in this large, spacious bathroom.

Ceramic wall tiles match the style and color of the floor tiles to create a neutral palette. This allows other design details, like the bamboo behind glass, to truly shine.

Accessories and other decorative items are displayed at eye level. These shallow shelves would also be good places to store clear containers of beauty supplies, such as cotton swabs, cotton balls, and sponges.

Place towel bars or hooks within 12" of sinks, tubs, and showers.

This centrally located towel bar serves both sinks. Here, the shared storage saves wall space and minimizes clutter.

Having a place for everything simplifies daily life.

Ergonomic experts tell us that the most useful storage space is between hip and shoulder height, yet the majority of bathroom storage is tucked under sinks and countertops. Not in this bathroom. Here, the double sinks are separated not merely by counter space, but by a shallow, pantry-like cabinet. Stored in an upper cabinet, grooming necessities can be reached without bending or stooping, which many of us appreciate first thing in the morning.

Trim molding surrounds the vanity area, framing it within the tall walls and high ceiling.

Brass door knobs and drawer pulls are coordinated with the brass fittings and accessories.

Simple molding complements the design of the raised panel doors and drawers as well as the elegance of the molding on the doors and walls of the room.

Cosmetics and medications need to be stored in cool, dark, dry places. Oddly enough, medicine cabinets rarely fit that description. In fact, medicine cabinets can be warm, humid environments. Think about it: they're often recessed, almost always above or adjacent to a sink, and typically surrounded by lights. Definitely not ideal. Reserve other, more appropriate places for your cosmetics and medications, and make sure medications are stored securely.

If there are children in your home, medications as well as cleaning supplies need to be completely inaccessible to them. Putting these items up out of reach isn't enough, either. Children have a way of reaching whatever captures their attention, and childproof caps aren't always childproof. Include a locking cabinet or fit a cabinet door or drawer with secure safety latches. Remember: lives depend on this.

 *Design*Wise

Pat Currier, CKD
Currier Kitchens & Baths
Amherst, New Hampshire

- There no longer seems to be a standard height for bathroom vanities. While 31" is typical, some master baths are implementing standard-height kitchen cabinets at 36". When selecting bathroom vanities, find a height that's comfortable for you and your family.

- Major manufacturers have begun using better products to treat vanities for the moist environments of bathrooms. Catalyzed-conversion varnishes and Thermofoil—a PVC film applied to fiberboard that imitates the look of paint— make cabinets downright water resistant.

- Function may be the most important consideration when selecting vanities and countertops. That vision of a beautiful marble counter topping an antique table may be perfect for a guest powder room, but impractical for daily grooming. Assess how your bathroom is most used, then look for materials that are best suited for that application.

- Laminate countertops are still the most cost-effective countertop material, and are now offered in a wider variety of colors and patterns than ever before. Many modern laminates also are available with scratch-resistant finishes.

Accentuate the positive.

Sections of cabinets unfurl against the curve of this wall, topped by a wood backsplash that emphasizes the room's graceful shape.

The elegant, curved trim on the backsplash complements the contrasting tones of the wood countertop. All the wood in this bathroom has been treated to high-quality sealers to protect it against water damage. Sealers of this sort need to be reapplied yearly in order to maintain their protection.

*Idea*Wise

t just can't be done: You can never have too much storage in a bathroom. Especially in small bathrooms, take every opportunity to add storage.

Frame an opening into a partition—or non-load-bearing wall—and trim it out with window casings.

Have glass shelves cut to fit the opening and install them on small cleats attached to the sides of the opening.

If privacy is an issue, fill the shelves with plants and other decorative items to block the view.

There's no rule that the main storage facilities have to surround the sink. Here, a simple tapered column supports the sink, which is flanked by a sleek line of drawers and a simple bench.

Extra storage is tucked into every possible space in this gleaming bathroom. One wall of the tub surround is converted to storage space by open shelves and cubby holes that hold wash cloths, soaps, candles, and cosmetic and beauty supplies. Nearby, hand and bath towels are kept fresh and dust free behind a glass door, and other, less attractive supplies are hidden by a raised-panel door.

Accessibility

Creating an accessible bathroom is mostly a matter of planning and consideration, which can make a bathroom more attractive and comfortable for the whole family. Consider these suggestions as you plan your bathroom cabinets and countertops:

• Add pull-down hardware to upper shelves (such as those in wall-mounted cabinets or medicine cabinets) to bring items into reach for seated people or those with limited mobility. Or, mount shelves or a medicine cabinet on the side of the sink rather than behind it to minimize reaching.

• Use fold-away doors, remove face frames on base cabinets, or install roll-out base cabinets to gain clear space beneath countertops.

• Provide clear space that is 29" high by 32 to 36" wide under sinks and lowered sections of countertop so seated users can comfortably reach the vanity.

• Vary the heights of the countertops to serve both standing and seated users.

• Conceal a pop-up step stool behind the toe-kick of a cabinet for the convenience of children and other small people.

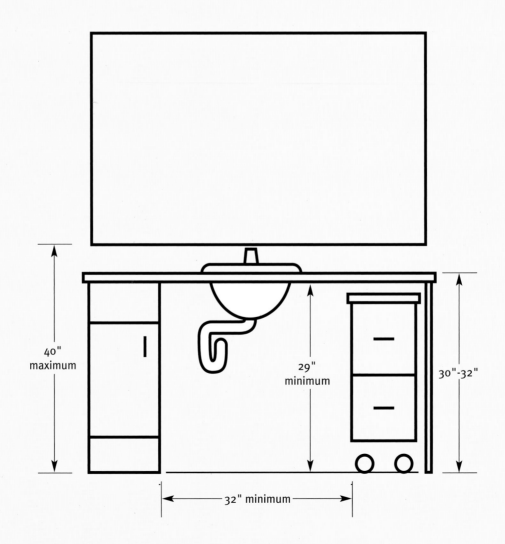

40" maximum

29" minimum

30"-32"

32" minimum

Accessibility doesn't have to announce itself.

This attractive, comfortable bathroom has been designed for maximum accessibility and efficiency for everybody.

Roll-out base cabinets provide seating space without sacrificing storage.

Easy-to-grip C-shaped pulls make drawers more accessible.

Bars attached to the front of the counter-tops allow seated users to pull themselves into position—and hold towels right where they're needed.

Insulated pipes pro-tect seated users from burns.

Placing the sink toward the front of the counter makes it easier to reach. (There should be no more than 21" from the front of the counter to the back of the sink.)

Including countertops and sinks at different heights creates accessible space for all users. Comfortable heights range from 32 to 43" for standing users and 30 to 34" for seated users.

In major remodeling projects or new construction, decide on locations and sizes for the towel bars early in the process so blocking can be installed before the drywall is hung.

Candles, bathing salts and a basket containing loofas, brushes, and other exfoliators rest on the ledge of the luxurious whirlpool, waiting for the next bather.

Teak, a durable hardwood, is at home in moist environments, such as bathrooms. This bench holds clothing and other items while family members bathe, and makes a great place to sit while changing clothes.

Towels, sponges, even soaps and candles are stored where they're used in this relaxed atmosphere.

By the way, if you haven't considered one before, now's the time: a towel warmer may be the ultimate luxury. These days, towel warmers can be found at surprisingly reasonable prices. Some are hard-wired into an available electrical circuit; others simply plug into a receptacle. Either way, you're in for a treat. Who wouldn't love wrapping themselves in a warm, fluffy towel on a cold day?

Transform necessities into accessories
by storing them in plain sight.

Large, bulky, or unat-
tractive items are hidden
behind closed doors in
the vanity cabinets.

Slightly obscured behind
textured glass doors, common objects such as a hand mirror,
pottery, and towels become decorative pieces in their own right.

Displaying towels attractively
isn't exactly fine art, but there is a
trick to it. For each stack, fold all
the towels in the same manner and
to the same size, then stack them
with all the folds facing the same
direction. This might sound trivial,
but try it. Details like this transform ordinary things into
extraordinary displays.

White on white on white might have become formless without the black border that defines the perimeter of the room and emphasizes the shape of the sink and storage pieces.

(above) A console table and sink can be nestled between stacks of drawers. In drawer stacks like these, store things according to how often you use them—place those used most often in the top drawer, least often in the bottom.

Take advantage of any open space around the sink. Here, a generous storage piece tucked between the sink and tub holds daily supplies and sports a towel ring for the sink.

Console-table sinks offer no real storage, which can present problems. If you love the style but think you can't sacrifice the storage offered by a vanity, think again. You may have more options than you first realize.

Make sure wood accessories are protected by water-resistant finishes.

Designers suggest storing towels within 12" of sinks, tubs, and showers. If your bathroom doesn't meet this guideline, fill in with accessories. Here, a simple set of wood shelves stores towels within reach of both the shower and the tub.

Countertops

Today's bathroom countertops can be anything from glass to wood to synthetics to concrete to natural stone. Ceramic tile also remains a favorite. Each material has its own strengths and weaknesses and each comes at a particular price. Some combine fantastic looks with fantastic prices; others combine reasonable prices with limitations regarding edge treatment and sink options. It's all a balancing act. In this case, you're balancing appearance, performance, and price.

It isn't important to choose a material that follows the trends of the moment, it's important to choose one that meets the needs of your family for each particular bathroom. The materials you'd choose for countertops in a family bath or children's bathroom may be quite different from what you'd select for a powder room near an entertainment area, for example.

It's also important to select countertops that complement other materials in the room. Generally, it's best to select your cabinets and flooring materials, then choose materials, colors, and textures for your countertops.

Remember that with most materials, matte finishes hide scratches better than glossy ones, and textured finishes are interesting but can be hard to keep clean.

Wood molding or special nosing covers the edges of laminate counters and adds a nice sense of style.

Solid-core laminate has color all the way through the body, which eliminates that issue. Solid-core is, however, more expensive and typically isn't available in as wide an array of colors and textures.

Plastic laminate has been a popular choice for decades because it's inexpensive, durable, and easy to maintain. Made of several layers of paper impregnated with phenolic resin and bonded by heat and pressure, the laminate itself is highly water resistant, but the substrate beneath isn't, so seams and sink cutouts have to be sealed thoroughly. The kraft-paper core of standard plastic laminate creates a dark line that can be seen on the edges.

Plastic laminate countertops scorch fairly easily—be careful with curling irons and other grooming appliances. It also can be scratched and chipped, but that typically isn't much of a problem in bathrooms.

Corners should be rounded for safety.

Solid-surface materials are one of the most popular countertop materials on the market. They're entirely water resistant and resist heat, marks, and scratches. The color goes all the way through, so minor scratches and marks easily can be sanded or polished away.

Solid-surface materials can be cut and shaped, which means they can be formed into interesting contours and given elaborate edge profiles. Here, an octagonal countertop crowns a vanity island. The malleability of solid-surface materials made it possible to cut the unusual countertop and form a pleasing, rounded profile on its edges.

The chief disadvantage of solid-surface material is the cost. Depending on the style, dimensions, and edge treatments you select, these countertops can be quite expensive. Only you can evaluate their value.

This faucet is fastened directly to the wall through the mirror to reflect the simple design of the unique curved double-vanity countertop.

Holes can be drilled to accommodate any faucet style.

Solid-surface materials can be shaped to fit almost any situation.

Below this striking countertop there is concealed storage. Accessible by sliding doors, the lack of trim and cabinet door knobs maintains this bathroom's sleek appearance.

The mosaic tile on this countertop produces an interesting coherence for the overall room design.

Tile is a perennial favorite for countertops and backsplashes because it's available in a vast range of sizes, styles, and colors; it's durable and can be repaired; some tile—not all—is reasonably priced.

Floor tile is the best choice for most countertops because it's harder and more durable than wall tile. Several types of tile, including glazed ceramic and porcelain tile as well as glass tile, make excellent countertops.

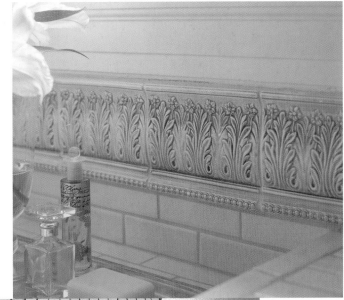

Mosaic glass tile covers this luminous countertop. Surrounding the sink with a contrasting color customizes the counter and gives it an extra splash of personality.

Speaking of splash, the backsplash here combines the two colors from the countertop with wavy liners, resulting in an all together pleasing arrangement.

One thing to keep in mind when choosing tile, especially small tile such as these, is that the many grout joints can create an uneven surface. This is less of an issue with large tile because they cover more space and, therefore, have fewer joints.

(right) Glass reveals countertops with great style. Here, a vessel sink rests atop a custom glass top. Installing a glass console table is another way to add glass counters to a bath.

To make a countertop, tempered glass—typically between ½ and 1" thick—is cut to size and then the edges are rounded and polished. These countertops are more practical than you might first think. Glass is nonporous, so it's stain proof and sanitary, the one-piece counter-tops have no dirt-and-grim catching seams, and tempered glass can support a surprising amount of weight.

Glass counters can be smooth, textured, etched, sandblasted, or patterned. Texture hides the surface scratches that glass can develop.

A custom glass top added to a vanity, such as this one, requires support beneath the cabinet.

(left) Concrete countertops can be formed into shapes from sleek to fanciful, such as the "banjo" vanity here. It requires adequate support and regular maintenance.

Daily cleaning is simple; most manufacturers recommend mild, nonabrasive, non-ammoniated soap. Regular maintenance is not quite as simple: concrete must be sealed initially and the sealer must be reapplied periodically.

Before committing to concrete countertops, discuss specific care recommendations with the manufac-turer or fabricator. Make sure you're comfortable with the ongoing commitment required by these outstanding countertops.

Natural stone enjoys tremendous popularity for good reason: It's elegant, most stone is easy to care for, and it's undeniably durable. Different varieties of stone have different characteristics and care requirements. Stone countertops give you the option of using undermount sinks, which have to be surrounded by finished, watertight edges.

With advances in protective sealers, wood has moved into the bathroom in new and surprising places, including countertops. Traditionally, most species of wood haven't mixed well with water, so the idea may be somewhat counterintuitive, but today's sealers make it practical as well as possible.

Here, thick planks have been shaped into a marquis-shaped countertop tailored to fit the curved wall that helps support it.

CHAPTER 3

Fixtures

What is it about warm water that so soothes our souls? After a good cry or before any major life transaction, we head to the sink to wash our faces, brush our teeth, and prepare ourselves for what lies ahead. And although a good shower or bath won't cure the common cold or solve life's major mysteries, we humans seem to feel better about it all after a good soak.

And so we must have sinks and tubs and showers suited to the purpose. And don't forget the toilet and possibly a bidet. Small wonder that bathrooms have grown larger—they had to in order to house our ever-larger array of fixtures. In the 1950s, the average bathroom was no bigger than 5 × 7 feet; today's master baths are often twice that size.

If you have the space, the question then becomes how to fill it. A toilet is, of course, a necessity, but what about a bidet? What is it and do you need or even want one? Is a whirlpool tub the ultimate luxury for you, or would a mammoth, multiple-head shower better suit your lifestyle and proclivities? How many sinks do you need and what style should they be?

No one can answer these questions for you, but this chapter showcases a range of available options and provides information to help you answer them for yourself. Maybe you should read it while soaking in the tub....

With so many options available, there's no reason to settle for hum-drum fixtures. Start with the basic realities—the dimensions of the room and the current locations of the plumbing—and let your imagination run as far as your space and budget allow.

If you're remodeling and plan to use an existing countertop, make sure you have the measurements of the countertop and cutout with you when shopping for a new sink. You can choose a sink that is the same size or larger as long as the plumbing remains in the same location.

A coatrack holds towels within reach of both the tub and shower.

A sliding showerhead lets users adjust the shower to varying heights.

Plumbing rises from the floor to serve this freestanding tub. Placing the faucets at the side of this tub allows bathers to rest comfortably against the end while enjoying the view.

Glass walls and doors have to be wiped down or squeegeed after every shower to keep them looking their best.

Vitreous china sinks are durable and nonporous, and easy to clean. Deep bowls reduce splashing.

The sinks, tubs, and showers in a bathroom should present a unified—but not necessarily matching—face to the world. Here, a contemporary glass shower sits among traditional-style fixtures and accessories, letting the room's abundant light move freely. A white-on-white color scheme, accented by deep wood tones, unifies the eclectic mix.

Sinks

Sinks are the most used fixture in any bathroom. Think about it: According to experts, the average person visits the bathroom six to eight times a day, and each of those visits includes (or certainly should) the obligatory trip to the sink; toothpaste commercials as well as our very own dentists encourage us to brush our teeth at least twice a day; we wash our hands before and after meals. You get the idea—sinks are part of our everyday lives, and they ought to be practical to use, attractive to look at, and accessible to every member of the family.

Many sinks, such as this one, are sold with pre-drilled holes for a faucet. Select a faucet that fits the hole pattern of the sink you've chosen—in this case, a single hole model.

Caulk seals the joint between the sink and countertop, preventing water damage.

Easy to install and often reasonably priced, self-rimming is the most popular style of sink. Here, a simple white sink is transformed into a striking piece with the addition of a unique ceramic faucet.

Free-standing sinks work in combination with wall-mounted faucets. With its basin resting atop a fanciful stand, this sink contributes high style as well as simple function. Lovely as it is, a sink such as this is best suited to a powder room or other lightly used bathroom rather than one in which multiple users get ready for each day.

 Words to the Wise

Sinks often are categorized according to how and where they are installed.

Vanity-mounted sinks are available in a range of styles:

Self-rimming sinks have rolled edges that rest directly on the countertop. This is typically the least expensive type of sink as well as the easiest to install. The drawback is that the joint between the sink and countertop attracts dirt and has to be cleaned regularly.

Flush-mounted sinks are recessed into the counter to sit flush with the surface. They blend nicely with countertops and are easy to keep clean. (A variation, tile-in sinks, is made to be used with tile countertops.)

Undermount sinks fit below the countertop. The edges of the countertop are exposed in this arrangements, so those edges have to be finished and watertight. For this reason, undermount sinks are often used with solid-surface or stone countertops.

Integral sinks are molded basins that are actually part of the countertops. Stainless steel and solid-surface countertops often include integral sinks, which are attractive, virtually seamless, and very expensive. Minor damage can usually be buffed out of these materials, but major damage means the whole unit has to be replaced, an expensive proposition.

Vessel sinks are reminiscent of the wash basins of years gone by. Each of these sinks rests above a small cut-out opening that is covered by the base of the vessel. They require surface- or wall-mounted faucets.

Vanity-top sinks rest above the countertop, appearing to be free-standing.

Wall-hung sinks are—as the name suggests—mounted directly to the wall at a comfortable height. They're highly useful in small bathrooms and in bathrooms designed for accessibility. Some models come with decorative shields to conceal the plumbing. Wall-hung sinks typically require special blocking between wall studs for structural support.

Pedestal and Free-standing sinks are attached to the wall and given additional support by the decorative bases on which they rest.

Pedestal sinks typically lack counterspace, but the generous deck of this sink provides a bit of room to work with as one prepares for the day. Hand towels rest on built-in towel bars and other sundries and supplies wait in a pantry-like cabinet.

Accessibility

To be accessible to seated users, a sink should be installed within 21" of the front edge of a countertop. When that's not possible, consider mounting the faucet controls at the side of the sink rather than the back. Or, choose a design that juts out past the counter's edge, which provides easy access from a seated position.

If you're shopping for an accessible sink, choose a style that's shallower at the front and deeper at the drain. When installing it, provide clear space that is 29" high by 32 to 36" wide beneath the sink and a lowered section of countertop.

*Idea*Wise

Vessel sinks are all the rage, but prices for some of those vessels are raging, too. If you want high style without the high prices, transform a simple waterproof vessel into a sink.

Cut a hole in the center of a vessel such as a laquerware, glass, or pottery bowl. Use a rotary cutter, a carbide bit, and a deft touch to cut the hole. If you're using laquerware, add several coats of laquer, letting it dry between coats.

Sandwich plumber's putty between the bowl and a drain body, and you've got a custom-made vessel sink on your hands.

Make sure there is at least 30" between double sinks, measured from centerline to centerline.

Who decided double sinks have to be identical?

If you can't decide between two sink styles, don't fret—choose both. Here, a raised vessel rests beside its counterpart, an under-mounted bowl. Both sinks and the countertops are solid-surface material, an elegant, practical material that can be fabricated into an almost infinite variety of shapes and sizes.

Like solid-surface countertops, solid-surface sinks are durable, easy to maintain, and clean up like a dream. If a sink becomes discolored, fill it with warm water, a little laundry detergent, and a small amount of chlorine bleach. Let the water soak until it's cool, then rinse the sink thoroughly.

Wall-mounted sinks are practical in bathrooms where accessibility is an issue or where space is at a premium. Here, a creamy wall-hung sink floats like a cloud against a sky blue wall, the supply pipes and drain concealed within the wall. Concealment isn't always possible, so plumbing shrouds are available to match most wall-hung sinks.

Wall-hung sinks require a fair amount of support. In major remodeling projects, decide on the location and height of the sinks early, and add blocking for wall-hung sinks before the drywall is hung. If the drywall is already in place, it's possible to cut away a section and add the necessary support.

Console-table sinks combine the space saving ways of pedestal sinks with a little bit of counterspace and a whole lot of style. A console table consists of a ledge surrounding a sink supported by the wall and at least two legs.

Console tables are available in many shapes, styles and colors. Some are offered with optional detachable shelves, towel rings, plumbing shrouds—even romantic fabric skirting.

Sinks can be installed in furniture pieces that have been adapted for the purpose. The chief requirement for this type of transformation is stability—in particular, a well supported countertop. With that in place, any style of sink can be added.

This vintage sideboard has been outfitted with an undermount sink and a marble countertop and backsplash. To accomplish this transformation, typically the top of the piece is removed. The sink is securely attached to the countertop, often with mounting strips, then the countertop is installed with corner braces and blocking.

Nontraditional materials find homes in today's bathrooms.

Stainless steel is. . .well. . .stainless, a fine attribute for a bathroom sink. Traditionally, stainless steel has been used more for kitchen sinks than for bathrooms, but current trends are changing that. After all, stainless steel hides dirt well; it's also durable and easy to clean. To produce this stain and corrosion resistant material, manufacturers combine stainless steel, chromium, and nickel.

The mirror finish on this console sink has to be treated gently—it scratches easily—so a sink like this would be most appropriate in a powder room or guest bath.

As long as holes can be drilled in the surrounding countertop, you can combine any style of faucet with an undermount sink.

Undermount sinks can be used only with countertops that have substantial waterproof edges, such as natural stone and solid-surface materials.

If your heart is set on a stainless steel sink in a heavily used bathroom, choose a satin finish. It doesn't show fingerprints or scratches as easily, and minor scratches can be buffed out with a scouring pad. Here, a stainless steel undermount sink is paired with a slate countertop, an interesting combination for the rustic setting.

Clearly elegant, glass sinks are surprisingly practical as well. They're scratch resistant, easy to clean, and—despite their fragile appearance—strong and durable. Even rapid changes in water temperature don't phase glass sinks.

Air bubbles that formed during the casting process give spun glass a pebbly surface that makes the sink interesting and inviting. And although the sink shown here is clear, colored glass is widely available.

To keep glass sinks looking their best, wipe them dry after use. Even when you're careful, spots left by the minerals in hard water are tough to avoid. If you don't have a water softener, add one. It will reduce the mineral content of the water and substantially reduce spotting.

Yes, that really is a wood sink and tub. The natural tones of the wood sink and tub positively glow against the deep green marble of the countertop, tub surround, and floor. It's not all that surprising—wood boats have been around for centuries. Properly maintained, this wood sink and tub will remain beautiful for a lifetime.

Bathtubs

Hip magazines and books continually preach about the restorative powers of warm water. From their pages, self-help gurus exhort us to wash our aches and pains—along with our cares and woes—down the drain as often as possible. For that you need a comfortable, attractive bathtub in a size, shape, and material that suits your bathroom and your family.

As you evaluate your options regarding the tub itself, there are other issues to consider. The first is size: You have to get the tub into the room and into position. Then, there are issues of structural support, plumbing, and—for a spa tub—wiring. And, no matter what your age or physical abilities, it's important to consider safety and accessibility when it comes to bathtubs.

The profile of the integral apron lends a sophisticated air to this classic tub.

The splash zone on alcove walls should be covered in water-resistant material, such as this elegant combination of marble and painted wood.

Alcove tubs are the most common type of tub for family bathrooms. These tubs are designed to fit into niches finished by walls on two or—more commonly—three sides. They're sold either with an integral or separate "apron" covering the exposed side of the tub.

Here, the tub is tucked into a three-sided alcove beneath a window. Having a window above a tub can be delightful—it provides wonderful light and ventilation—but when it's at the business end of the tub it complicates the placement of plumbing. In this alcove, that problem was neatly solved by adding a bumped-out wall to house the plumbing.

Alcove tubs with only one side apron are sold as either "left-hand" or "right-hand" models, depending on the location of the predrilled drain and overflow holes in the tub. To determine which type you need, face into the alcove and determine whether the tub drain is (or will be) on your right or left.

Tub and shower combinations pack a lot of options into small spaces. Here, a one-piece module includes both a tub and shower. The walls of the tub surround were specially molded to give the appearance of ceramic tile and to provide space for towels and other bathing necessities.

To prevent scalding, tub and shower control valves must be pressure balanced, thermostatic mixing, or a combination of those types.

 ## Words to the Wise

Tubs are manufactured from a variety materials, each with its own set of advantages and disadvantages.

Fiberglass is an inexpensive, lightweight material available in many colors. It is easily molded, so tub units can be formed to include seats, grab bars, and other conveniences. The surface of fiberglass scratches easily and its color fades over time.

Acrylic, like fiberglass, can be molded into just about any size and shape. Unlike fiberglass, however, the color runs through the entire substance rather than just the surface coat, making it less likely to fade or develop scratches.

Enameled steel tubs are shaped from sheets of steel and coated with a baked-on enamel similar to that of cast-iron tubs. However, the enamel layer usually is thin and susceptible to chipping. In addition, enameled steel doesn't retain heat and tends to be noisy.

When buying an enameled steel tub, make sure it has an undercoating designed to muffle sound and retain heat.

Cast iron is the toughest material available for tubs. The iron is cast into a tub shape then coated with a baked-on enamel that is relatively thick (1/16"), resulting in a richly colored finish. The enamel is strong, durable, and very resistant to chips, scratches, and stains. The cast iron itself is almost impervious to dents and cracks. Cast iron is just about indestructible, and it's also heavy—a standard tub weighs between 300 and 400 pounds. Often the floor framing must be reinforced to support the additional weight. Cast iron is used most commonly for claw-foot and other free-standing tubs.

Deck-mounted tubs and whirlpools rest on the subfloor and are surrounded by custom-built decks or platforms. Here, tile covers the deck and surrounding walls, creating a spa atmosphere.

Typically, deck-mounted and platform tubs have a larger capacity than standard tubs and a more luxurious feel. Although the tubs themselves are priced much like alcove tubs, the construction of the deck or platform can add a significant amount to the total cost.

Before adding a tub configuration like this in a remodeling project, make sure the floor will support its weight. Replace existing floor joists beneath the tub if they're damaged, too small, or too far apart. Generally, you'll need to add support under the tub area if the current joists are 2×10 or smaller, or if they're more than 16" apart. If you have questions about support issues, contact a building inspector or professional contractor.

Light fixtures above tubs must be vapor-proof and carry a UL rating for wet areas.

This deck-mounted tub is surrounded by ocean-blue tile and a glass-block shower in a serene dream of a bathroom. Classic cream-colored fixtures are combined with water-colored tones in a number of textures to form a decorating scheme that will remain fresh and inviting for decades.

For many people, a spa tub is the ultimate bathroom luxury. And while these tubs are undeniably relaxing and enjoyable, adding one to a bathroom is not entirely simple.

Before you choose a spa tub, talk with your designer, contractor, or a local building inspector to make sure you understand all the ramifications of that choice. Once you have a firm grasp on the requirements and expenses involved, if those tiny bubbles are still calling you, go for it!

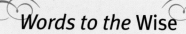

Words to the Wise

Hot tubs recirculate water alone.

Whirlpool tubs pump a combination of air and water through a series of jets. They require access to the pumps and other plumbing as well as frequent and thorough cleaning.

Air jet tubs pump warm water into the tub. Water doesn't circulate through the pipes, so there's no issue of standing water in the pipes and no need for additional plumbing access.

If bathing avec deux is what you have in mind, choose a large-capacity tub and place the spout in the middle so both people can relax comfortably against an end. Position the water controls and faucet toward the outside edge of the tub at a height of 38 to 48" so the water can be turned on and adjusted before you get into the tub…and after.

Use your imagination: Tubs don't always have to be set into niches or alcoves. Deck-mounted tubs can be set as peninsulas or even stand alone in the center of a room.

The placement of this spa tub in combination with the stunning copper tile surrounding the deck make it the centerpiece of the room. Its extra depth and comforting jets make it a pleasure to own and use.

A spa tub holds 50 to 100 gallons of water, which means you may need a large capacity hot water heater and extra support for the floor.

Adding two faucets lets you fill large-capacity tubs more quickly. High-flow valves have an increased flow rate that speeds up the process, too.

Steps surrounding a tub can be dangerous. Make sure the floor covering is extremely slip resistant.

To get the effect of a sunken tub without the dangers, raise the tub on a platform and surround it with space to walk or sit. Here, the tub is sunk into a generous platform with a spectacular view.

Freestanding tubs can be located any place that can be reached by supply lines and drain lines. Supported by wooden braces, this tub stands in front of a bank of floor-to-ceiling windows, giving bathers a doubly luxurious experience.

The panels and ledge of this handsome, custom-built tub are concrete, a material that's tailor-made for contemporary settings such as this.

Not every bathroom can accommodate such a tub—the weight of the concrete alone requires a substantial amount of support in the floor. In fact, some extremely heavy tubs may not be practical on the second floor of a wood-framed house. Contact a professional contractor or building inspector if you have questions about structural support.

Dropping the ceiling over the tub suggests the intimacy of an enclosure without limiting the space in any way.

Sheer curtains can be drawn to obscure the tub from the rest of the room without completely blocking the light or the view.

(below) Tile and stone can be used to build custom tubs in unusual shapes and sizes. Here, dramatic thick porcelain tile is shaped into a simple but elegant soaking tub.

The floor of a custom-made tub is built with floor mortar (or "deck mud"), and must slope toward the drain a minimum of one-quarter inch for every 12 inches.

*Dollar*Wise

If you love the look of claw-foot tubs but not their prices, go treasure hunting. Many salvage yards and reuse centers carry vintage cast iron tubs at reasonable prices.

The next step is to find a good refinisher. Get a referral from someone you know and trust or contact several references from prospective contractors. A good refinishing job will last for decades, but an incorrectly finished tub can chip within months.

Have the interior of the tub refinished and paint the exterior.

Showers

According to trend watchers and other keepers of home design statistics, elaborate showers have overtaken whirlpools as the luxury-of-choice for today's bathrooms. Many of the people who bought enormous whirlpool tubs in the previous decade found that they simply didn't have the time necessary to fill or clean them adequately. Enter the instant gratification of the luxury shower, today's answer to the age-old cry for "Serenity Now."

Today's showers range from the economical efficiency of a tub and shower combination to the all-out decadence of the total body spa, and everything in between. The best shower for your bathroom is one that fits the space available, your budget, and your lifestyle.

Plumbing in a wet wall like this can supply the shower as well as a sink on the other side of the wall.

The multitude of grout lines in mosaic tile gives it superior slip resistance.

Repeating the design motif here calls attention to the shower's curb and reduces the likelihood of tripping over it.

Mosaic glass tile makes an outstanding shower. Here, tile walls and floors surround the shower, relieving any concern about splashing beyond the open shower. In large showers like this, rubber membrane covers the substrate to improve its water resistance.

Simple tile mosaics provide points of interest within the strong color of this tile shower. The tiled niche and bench make it functional as well as beautiful.

Shower benches offer seating for those who shave in the shower as well as for those who tire easily. Benches should be about 18" high and at least 15" deep.

A sliding shower head like this can be adjusted to the right height for each member of the family.

Water tends to puddle in enclosed spaces. To avoid mildew, wipe niches dry after the day's last shower.

Including a variety of shower-heads at a variety of heights makes a shower convenient and comfortable for everyone in the family.

Something for every body.

Lights inside showers must be vapor-proof and rated for use in wet areas.

Two showerheads produce twice the moisture. The ventilation system must be designed to handle the load.

Glass walls and doors need to be wiped down after each shower to avoid mineral spots and soap scum.

The rimless shower doors have no trim to develop mold or mildew. The wide threshold slants into the shower to direct water toward the drain.

Handheld showers are convenient for people in a hurry as well as children and other smaller users.

Large-capacity showers sometimes require special drains as well as 1" supply pipes.

Rain-head showers produce delightful deluges when you have the time to indulge yourself and to get your hair wet. For most of us though, there are times when we need to get in and out of the shower quickly with as little fuss as possible. Enter the hand-held shower head.

With two rain heads and a generous enclosure, this shower easily accommodates two people. Double showers sometimes can be efficient and they certainly can be fun.

This self-cleaning threshold guides water and soap residue to the sloped clean-out feature where it can be wiped away or naturally channeled to the drain.

Convenient features, such as seats and ledges, are molded into many shower modules. This fiberglass-reinforced acrylic shower module features a high domed ceiling, sculpted ledges, and a removable seat.

Most shower modules are available in one-piece or multi-piece units. One-piece units have no seams and are easy to install, but multi-piece units are easier to maneuver through doorways and up staircases as is often necessary in remodeling projects. Seams should be discreet rather than easily visible and should be designed to create watertight seals after installation.

*Design*Wise

Linda Burkhardt
Kitchens & Baths by Linda
Montauk, NY

SHOWERS:

- A built-in shower seat is essential to any custom shower. It's the perfect place to perch and pedicure!

- Glass tiles, natural stones and handmade ceramics are luxury materials to incorporate in bathroom design. If working on a budget, a little bit of luxury material can go a long way. Consider running a band around the shower, adding color in a niche, or topping off a bath with ceramic crown molding.

- For bathrooms with limited space, consider pedestal sinks with ample surface space for necessities. This maximizes floor space and gives the illusion of a bigger room. For a tailored look, consider sinks or pedestals with a rectangular shape.

SINKS:

- Powder room sinks are a great place to reflect your personal style. Whether it's a vessel sink floating on a stone slab, a hand painted basin perched on a flea-market console, or a minimalist modern pedestal, express yourself!

- When selecting materials, consider white porcelain—it's timeless and always more cost effective than fashion colors.

- Undermounted sinks create a clean and uncluttered look, focusing attention on decorative elements. This high-end detail works well in both contemporary and traditional designs.

TUBS:

- With today's busy lifestyles, a soaking tub in a master suite is a great way to create your own personal spa.

- Tub-shower combinations are commonplace in today's homes. Look beyond shallow standard tubs, and consider those that are deeper and wider. To gain more elbowroom in a typical tub-shower, use a curved shower rod.

Solid-surface material showers are attractive and easy care. Prefabricated models have curved corners and smooth surfaces, which eliminate hard-to-clean crevices and grout lines. These modules are available with built-in shelves and ledges, and can be installed directly over existing tile as long as it's sound and securely attached to the wall material.

Solid-surface panels in ¼ and ⅛" thicknesses can be used to create custom-built showers.

Either way, you get the advantages of solid-surface materials—their finish resists stains and water spotting, cleans up easily, and can be buffed to remove small scratches and stains.

Glass block walls make bright, interesting showers. Here, glass block is combined with tile in a large, innovative shower.

Using a wide opening rather than a door is trendy right now, but may or may not be practical, depending on your family and circumstances. A wide, curbless opening like this makes the shower highly accessible, but the floor beyond the opening must be water- and slip-resistant in order to be safe.

Multi-head shower and body spas require full enclosures and plenty of ventilation. Here, the glass walls and doors extend to the ceiling to contain the warmth as well as the energetic splashing of the water.

Tile protects the ceiling.

Operable windows provide welcome light and ventilation in shower enclosures.

A towel bar or hook should be located within 22" of the shower opening.

Accessible Tubs & Showers

Building an accessible shower is mostly a matter of careful planning and attention to detail. Wide, curbless openings, gently sloping floors, adjustable showerheads, and shower seats combine to create showers that everyone can use and enjoy.

A tile design takes the place of rugs, which present tripping hazards and make it difficult for wheelchairs to maneuver.

(below) An alcove shower with an adjustable height showerhead is comfortable for everyone. The sliding bar can be positioned at heights to fit adults of every size, children, and seated users.

Grab bars help users steady themselves on slippery surfaces and support people transferring to a shower or tub from a wheelchair or walker. Here, brass grab bars match the finish on the door handles, controls, and showerheads.

Universal design specialists and the ADA guidelines suggest placing a horizontal grab bar on the control wall, 24" long and 34 to 38" above the floor. The side wall should include a bar 32 to 48" long and 34 to 38" above the floor.

Grab bars must be attached to studs or installed with anchors rated to support at least 300 pounds each.

Shower doors should open into the room so they can't be blocked by someone who has fallen or otherwise needs assistance.

A seat next to the handheld showerhead is convenient for seated users and people who shave in the shower.

Molded supports hold grab bars securely.

Transfer seats make transferring into and out of the tub easier.

Tub and shower combinations offer accessible bathing options in limited space. Tubs designed for accessibility have slip-resistant bottoms and grab bars placed to support users as they shower or transfer into and out of the tub. Tub/shower modules are available in one- and two-piece units.

Toilets and Bidets

Toilets probably aren't anyone's favorite topic of conversation, but there's a lot to consider when purchasing and placing a toilet.

First, there's style. One-piece toilets are streamlined and seamless—the tank and bowl are integrated. Two-piece toilets have separate tanks and bowls connected with bolts. They're easier to install but typically more bulky.

Then there's shape. Elongated bowl are more comfortable for adults, but they take up more space than round-front bowls. Round bowls can be easier for small children to use. Compact elongated toilets enable a longer bowl to fit in smaller spaces.

And don't forget flushing systems. Reductions in water flow have reduced the power of the flush, which has spawned a variety of technologies designed to produce clean, quiet flushes.

Finally, there's the big question about placement. Should the toilet (and bidet, if there is one) be open to the rest of the room or have its own compartment? There's no one right answer of course. The best choice depends on the space available, the size and shapes of those who use the bathroom on a regular basis.

A bidet basically is a sit-down washbasin. Some consider bidets more hygienic than toilet paper. For those of you who always wanted to know but were afraid to ask, the user sits over the bowl, facing the faucet to control the spray or fill the bowl with water.

Design standards suggest 18" from the centerline of the toilet to the nearest fixture, wall, or other obstruction.

Gravity-fed, two-piece toilets with taller, thinner tanks have improved flushing power.

One-piece toilets, with their simpler lines, often complement contemporary settings. In bathrooms where space is at a premium, they often can fit under an extension of the vanity counter.

Although two-piece toilets usually are sold without seats, a one-piece toilet often comes with a seat designed to complement the lines of the design of the toilet.

Place a toilet paper holder 8 to 12" in front of the toilet bowl, 26" above the floor

Pressure-assisted toilets like this one can save an average of 2,000 gallons of water a year for a typical family.

For some families, space is enough of a separation between the vanity area and toilet. Here, a large but open area hosts both the toilet and bidet, while the remaining fixtures sit out of the direct line of sight.

For those who prefer a measure of privacy but feel claustrophobic in a small compartment, a partial wall topped by textured glass is an appealing option.

Towel bars make wise use of the space above the toilet without interfering with the user's comfort.

Space-efficient pocket doors slide completely out of view when not needed.

For more modest folks, only a separate compartment is truly comfortable. Here, a translucent sliding door provides privacy without blocking the light.

Bidets typically are placed near a toilet in order to share the plumbing and drain lines. Choose a toilet and bidet from the same design group or at least ones that share complementary design lines in order to coordinate the two.

A bidet requires the same space and clearance as a toilet, approximately 48 × 48" of floor space from the front edge to any wall or fixture. Plumbing codes are quite specific with regard to the placement of toilets and bidets—check with your designer, contractor, or local code before committing to a plan for your bathroom.

The shower, bidet, and sink are collected along a wall in this bathroom and the toilet sits modestly in a separate compartment, a perfectly reasonable set-up.

Horizontal spray bidets, with their directionally adjustable sprays, are better for front side cleaning. Vertical sprays, with water that sprays from the bottom of the fixture or fills the basin from above, are better for back side cleaning.

For the sake of convenience, make sure towels are available near the bidet. Here, separate towel bars serve the shower and bidet and the frame of the console sink holds towels for the sink.

Elevated toilets are comfortable for taller users and those who have difficulty sitting down or rising from a seated position. Here, the toilet is placed on a ledge, effectively elevating it.

Taller toilets, sometimes referred to as "comfort-height" are widely available. These toilets, about as tall as a chair, are comfortable for any average-sized adult. Children and smaller users appreciate standard toilets, which are between 15 and 16" tall.

Grab bars make it safer and easier to use a toilet. ADA guidelines and universal design specialists recommend placing a horizontal bar at one side, between 42" to 12 ft. long, 33 to 36" above the floor. They further recommend a grab bar on the wall behind the toilet, 24" to 6 ft. long, 33 to 36" above the floor.

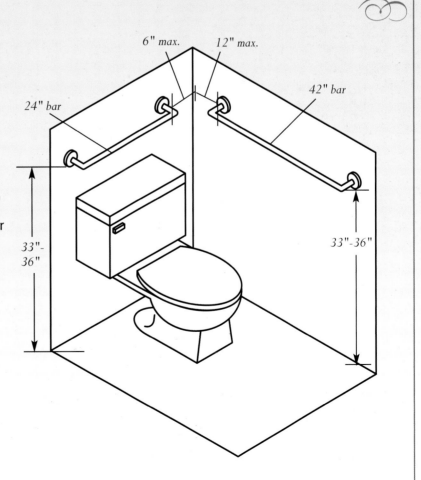

CHAPTER 4

Fittings

Fixtures and fittings—faucets, spouts, showerheads, and the like—are sold separately, but they're actually interdependent parts of a whole and have to be compatible with one another. If, for example, you've chosen a single-hole sink, you simply must choose a single-handled faucet. If you've fallen for a large whirlpool, a high-capacity bath valve will fill it faster and help you fit enjoyment of it into your schedule more often.

Compatibility is the most obvious issue when it comes to selecting fittings. Once you know the fitting works with the fixture, you're faced with decisions regarding styles, finishes, and valves, just to name a few. Take some time with these decisions—well-made fittings are virtually indestructible but can be expensive, and some gorgeous pieces require more care than you may be willing to invest. The best fitting is one that suits your bathroom, your budget, and your lifestyle.

Throughout this chapter you'll see fittings in a range of sizes, styles, and finishes. Pay attention not only to the fittings you like but the fixtures that complement them, and you'll be ready to dive right into selecting your own.

Fantastic fittings complete this picture-perfect bathroom.

The simple chrome towel bar and
low-voltage light fixture suit the
style and tone of the fittings.

Hand-held showerheads are convenient
for users of all heights and abilities.

A two-handled, deck-mounted faucet and
spout are positioned so they can be reached
from outside or inside the tub.

Chrome, single-handle faucets are extremely
popular because they're easy to use and easy
to maintain. These long spouts extend well
into the deep basins.

Sleek chrome fittings gleam in this contemporary setting. Each piece
was chosen to suit the fixture it serves and to contribute to the overall picture. The two-handled
tub fixture complements the single-handle sink faucets without being an identical match.

This bathroom clearly has been designed in accordance with universal design principals.
A hand-held showerhead, easy-to-use faucet handles, clear spaces beneath the sinks, accessible
storage, and a curbless shower welcome users of all abilities.

Sink Faucets

Like the right tie with a sharp suit or the perfect accessories with a stunning dress, a faucet enhances the appearance of a sink. The size, shape, style, and finish of each should complement the other.

The two factors that most affect faucet style are the number of handles and the shape and length of the spout. Traditional-style faucets have two handles while more contemporary-looking faucets often have one. Transitional styles work in many settings.

Once you've chosen a style, examine the construction and finish of the faucets you're considering. Generally, a well-made faucet will feel solid in your hands. The most durable faucets have solid-brass construction, corrosion-resistant finishes, and ceramic disc valves.

Mounted on a mirrored wall, these fittings seem to float above the spun glass bowl of a sink. Wall-mounted faucets are used in combination with sinks that don't have holes, such as vessel and under-mount sinks. Separate wall-mount valves and drains complete their installation.

Lever handles are easy to use, especially for people with limited hand strength. The arching design of this wide-spread faucet makes it delightfully attractive as well.

The tall, curved neck of this crescent faucet adds a bit of flair to the subtle elegance of this bathroom. Crescent, or gooseneck, faucets are best paired with deep basins that contain the fall of the water without excessive splashing.

*Idea*Wise

In extremely rustic or extremely contemporary settings, the water supply system can supply the fittings as well. Half-inch copper pipe, gate valves, and support brackets, typically used for rough plumbing, can be configured to deliver water right to a bathroom sink.

You can design a configuration to suit the space and sink, but here's the basic idea: Extend the hot and cold supply pipes to an opening at the center of the sink. In a convenient spot on each side, install a gate valve to control the flow of water.

Note: This high-concept idea may not be practical in homes that include children or adults with limited hand strength.

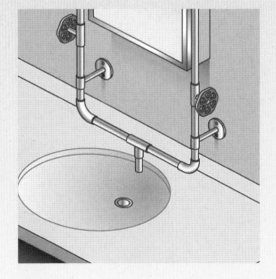

Brass fittings traditionally have been considered attractive but high maintenance because unprotected brass oxidizes when exposed to air. The protective lacquer and epoxy coatings developed to solve the problem were only partially successful because few of them stood up well to daily cleaning, especially abrasives.

New technology has been developed to give brass a finish that's as durable and easy to care for as chrome. Ask your designer, contractor, or retailer to make sure the fittings you're considering have the most durable finish possible.

Here, wide-spread brass sink and tub faucets glow against a neutral background.

Wide-spread faucets have two handles separate from the spout. Their size balances well with larger sinks and the space between pieces makes them easy to clean.

Powder-coated epoxy finishes are long lasting, easy to clean, and available in a variety of colors. Here, a white faucet virtually becomes part of a clean-lined pedestal sink.

Tub Faucets & Showerheads

Tub faucets and showerheads have contributions to make to the style of a bathroom, but their selection is fairly well determined by the selection of the sink faucets. However, there's still much to consider: placement, accessories, and—above all—safety.

Most building codes have requirements regarding scald protection on tub and shower fittings, and for good reason. Every day, in the United States alone, 300 young children are treated for burns resulting from hot water.

The reasons are not mysterious. Most manufacturers ship water heaters set at 140 to 150° F, and despite frequent warnings, many homeowners don't turn them down to the 120° F recommended by the National Safety Council. It takes only five seconds for a child to receive third-degree burns from water at 140°; two seconds at 150°.

The message here? Set your water heater at 120° F; replace any old valves with pressure-balancing valves that protect users from drastic temperature changes if someone flushes a toilet or runs water elsewhere in the house; if your household includes young children or elderly people, add safety-stop devices to your tub and shower faucets to limit how hot they can be set. And, of course, never leave young children unattended in a bathtub or shower.

Elegant and sleek, this deck-mounted faucet pours forth the soothing magic of warm water into a deep whirlpool tub. When choosing a deck-mounted faucet, make sure its reach is adequate and its size proportional to the setting.

The graceful curves of these crescent spouts soften the angular lines of the counter and bath deck. The matching accessories are nice finishing touches for the room.

Fittings should be mounted on the side of tubs meant for two. That way, both ends of the tub offer plenty of room to lie back and relax.

Handsprays are wonderful conveniences for tubs. They're handy for washing a child's hair (or your own), as well as for rinsing the tub itself.

*Design*Wise

Trudy McCollum ASID, CKD, CBD

Kitchen and Bath Ideas
North Little Rock, AR

- There are a number of exciting new faucet finishes on the market today that will bring a sense of elegance and sophistication to your bathroom, including weathered copper, pewter, and black, French, or oil-rubbed bronze.

- Coordinate your cabinet pulls and knobs, towel bars and light fixtures with faucet finishes to bring an updated and unified look to your bathroom. And don't overlook the small items like toilet levers and the exposed stops, supply pipes, and P-traps of pedestal sinks. The details make the difference!

- Create a "mini spa" experience easily and inexpensively by swapping out your standard showerhead for a massage or rainspout showerhead. These fittings are now available with all the hardware you need to connect to the existing, standard plumbing.

- All retrofit tub and shower faucets must contain an anti-scald device, such as a pressure-balance valve, to protect bathers from being scalded by hot water or blasted with cold water when another fixture or appliance is in use.

Tub and shower combinations share water lines. A diverter valve directs water to either the tub spout or the showerhead. This space-saving combination is especially popular in children's and family baths.

This shower has something for everyone: a tall fixed head and an adjustable, hand-held head. Unlike many similar combinations, these heads are controlled independently and so could be run at the same time.

This is more than a shower, it's a watery world of its own.
Often called body spas, units like this include a showerhead as well as high-volume jets aimed for your head, neck, and lower back. In many such systems, the water is collected in the basin and recirculated, but they still require high-capacity water heaters, supply lines, and drains.

DollarWise

Tall faucets designed for deep or vessel sinks can be quite expensive because they're quite trendy. Kitchen faucets, which are similar but have been around for ages, often are less expensive and just as practical.

Find a kitchen faucet in a size that balances well with your sink and chances are, it will be less expensive than a similar faucet marketed specifically for bathrooms.

CHAPTER 5

Lighting & Ventilation

Too often, bathroom lighting is merely an afterthought, purchased with whatever is left over in the budget after the surfaces, fixtures, and fittings are in place.

Big mistake. Huge. Good lighting makes bathrooms look better, but what may be more important is that good lighting makes us look better. For most of us, whatever time we spend reflecting on our reflections is spent in the bathroom. Shouldn't we cast the most flattering, color-correct light possible onto ourselves and our grooming routines?

Good bathroom lighting is more than mere vanity, though. Lighting actually can be a safety issue as well. Everyone—young and old—is less likely to fall or otherwise injure themselves in a well-lit room, especially if the light is set to reveal thresholds, steps, and areas that might be wet or slippery.

Like beauty, adequate lighting levels are in the eye of the beholder. Literally: The lenses of our eyes thicken and yellow as we age, so that by the age of 55, our eyes require twice as much light as they did at 20. Make an effort to create a lighting design that works for every member of the family today and well into the future.

Ventilation, another health and safety issue, is fundamental to bathrooms and should be designed into the plan from the very beginning of a project. Operable windows and mechanical ventilation improve the air we breathe and protect the structure itself from excess moisture.

Good bathroom lighting plans illuminate and enhance the features of the room as well as the features of the people who use the room. No one light source can accomplish such a feat—it takes layers of light produced by carefully planned and placed fixtures.

Natural and artificial light play off one another beautifully.

Skylights provide natural light from above. Some skylights, controlled by remote, also provide ventilation.

Vanity lighting is all about lighting the face, not the room. The best vanity lights are hung at eye-level on the side of the mirror.

These blinds can be closed for privacy, but windows provide both light and ventilation when desired. Whenever possible, at least 10 percent of a bathroom's light should be natural light.

Lampshades soften glare and cast more flattering light than bare bulbs or even globes.

Mirrors reflect and multiply light.

The skylight, windows, mirrors, and fixtures of this tropical themed bathroom team up to produce an effective, attractive lighting scheme.

Aim the beams at the outside edge of the tub to create pleasant, nonglare light for bathing.

Overhead fixtures provide the main source of light in the room.

(above) Recessed lights are not ideal as the main light source in a bathroom, but as supplemental sources, they positively shine. Here, recessed lights provide task lighting for specific areas such as the tub and toilet. To reduce glare and shadows, angle the bulbs to bounce off walls and ceilings.

Accent lighting draws attention to interesting architectural and structural features.

Here, rope lighting behind cove molding highlights the molding and curved ceiling.

*Design*Wise

Jeff Livingston, LS
& Deborah Foucher Stuke, CLC
Luce Design Group
Manchester, NH

- A single source of light cannot perform all your lighting needs. Layer ambient, task, decorative, and accent light to create a properly illuminated room.

- Lighting should surround the face at the mirror. Fixtures placed 30 to 36" apart on the vertical plane provide even illumination and minimize shadows. Mounting heights vary depending on the fixture style and ceiling heights, but normally are centered at about 66" off the finished floor. For added interest, mount fixtures through the mirror. Avoid downlighting over the mirror as the only source lighting the face.

- Skin tones look best in warm light. Use incandescent sources or fluorescent sources with a color temperature of 3500K or less.

- Use dimming controls to provide variable light levels. Many dimmers have a "soft start" feature, which slowly raises the light level over a period of seconds to allow eyes to adjust to the light. A slow fade to "on" is nice for nighttime bathroom visits!

- Choose decorative fixtures with translucent lenses. Avoid clear glass, which produces glare, and colored glass, which will change the color of light reflecting on your face.

- Proper ventilation ensures healthy indoor air quality. The fan you select should be rated for the size of your room. To calculate the proper CFM (cubic feet per minute), multiply the square footage by 1.1 if the ceiling height is 8 feet. For ceilings over 8 feet, multiply the ceiling height by .1375, then multiply the square feet to determine the required CFM. Select a fan with at least this rating.

- Few things are more annoying in a bathroom than a noisy vent fan. Consider the noise (measured in sones) generated by the unit. One sone or less is recommended. Features such as timers, occupancy sensors, and humidity sensors are available for added comfort and convenience.

Vertical fluorescent fixtures

eliminate shadows when fitted with color-correct, full-spectrum bulbs. Here, the center of each fixture is positioned at eye level in order to cast flattering light across the face of a person using the sink.

The vanity fixtures should be spaced to illuminate both sides of the face equally, typically three to four feet apart.

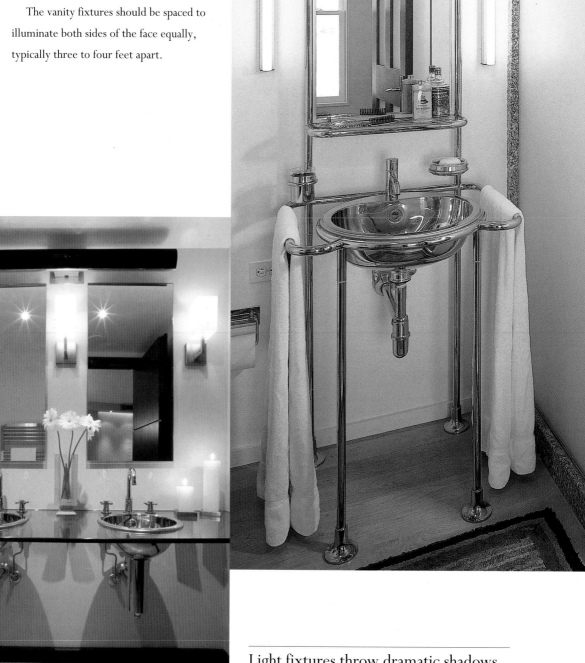

Light fixtures throw dramatic shadows

through the clear glass of this countertop. To reduce shadows in the mirrors, each is illuminated from three directions: above, to the left, and to the right.

Mirror, mirror on the wall: What's the most flattering light of all?

Amber globes cast warm light akin to candlelight onto this powder-room mirror. The incandescent light above the mirror balances the color and reduces shadows.

Unique lighting fixtures like this are appealing in a powder room, but colored globes are not always ideal in a master or main family bathroom. In those bathrooms, frosted or clear textured glass provides better light for daily grooming routines.

Coordinating the light fixtures with the other fixtures in the room creates a heightened sense of style. The elliptical stainless steel sink, curved chrome faucet fittings, and arched arms of the light fixture go well together without exactly matching. Shopping for coordinated pieces makes a room more interesting and reflects more of your own personal taste than selecting pieces from a matching suite.

Strip lights above mirrors are extremely popular because they're inexpensive and low maintenance. They do not, however, always offer the most flattering light. If you choose strip lighting, reduce the glare by using frosted rather than clear bulbs.

*Idea*Wise

Read any magazine article or book on stress reduction these days, and you're bound to find that the list of prescribed cures includes long, relaxing soaks in a hot bath. If your idea of relaxing in the tub includes reading that magazine or book, you're going to need some light. Still, the glare of overhead lights may not be what you have in mind.

Install a small sconce or hard-wired library light on the side wall of the tub enclosure, on the end opposite the spout. Place the switch outside the tub enclosure, well out of reach so you won't be tempted to switch on the light while seated in the tub. Remember: Electricity and water DO NOT mix.

*Shades cast more flattering light
than bare bulbs. Frosted glass
softens glare and shadows.*

*Full-spectrum light bulbs let you
see in the mirror what others will
see in the daylight.*

*Heat dissipates from the sockets of
bulbs that face down, so bulbs tend
to last longer.*

*Lamps must be placed far from
sinks and other water sources and
should be plugged into GFCI-
protected receptacles.*

(above) Lighting a dressing table mirror can be quite a
challenge. In a large area such as this, sconces would be too far apart to
provide adequate light, but strip fixtures above mirrors can produce glare and
unflattering shadows. These homeowners solved the puzzle by using frosted
globes on lights that face down rather than out, and by adding countertop lamps.

Dimmers are a good idea in every bathroom, but especially in a situation like
this. Here, the fixtures can be dimmed and the lamps turned on for a softer,
more relaxing atmosphere.

Whenever possible, natural light sources should contribute 10 percent of a room's ambient, or general, light. Get creative with glass block, traditional, or tubular skylights, and funky window combinations.

Operable windows topped by stationary transoms sparkle above a spacious soaking tub. These windows provide ventilation as well as light, since they can be opened to let moisture out and fresh air in.

It's a bit of a stretch, but these handles can be reached over the tub and bathers can easily reach them while seated in the tub. When choosing windows, consider their style of operation as well as their design style.

Let the sun shine in.

Bathroom windows present a challenge when it comes to window treatments. Some options are extremely expensive and others just aren't suited to a moist environment. Still, most of us are reluctant to leave bathroom windows completely uncovered, especially in neighborhoods where the houses are close together.

To provide privacy simply and inexpensively, buy an acid-etching kit at a craft store and etch the glass in a modesty zone on each window. If you're creative and imaginative you can do designs; if not, just etch a broad band or the whole window. Read and follow the manufacturer's directions carefully—these products can be caustic.

Tubular skylights deliver abundant natural light, a wonderful commodity in a bathroom that doesn't have other windows. The bathroom shown here includes a beautiful bank of windows in addition to the skylight, but many bathrooms don't include such riches.

Tubular skylights are reasonably priced and energy-efficient. Since they don't require any complicated framing, they're also easy to install. Some manufacturers use flexible plastic tubing that can be snaked around attic obstructions; others use solid plastic reflecting tubes that require more clearance. Evaluate your attic and roof as well as a range of these products before making a choice.

(right) The ideal lighting scheme combines natural and artificial light sources at a number of levels. Here, large windows provide natural light, a sconce provides light at eye level, and a fixture above the mirror provides task lighting. Shutters filter the natural light; frosted globes on the fixtures reduce glare as well.

An exhaust system provides mechanical ventilation for the room. In a heavily-used bathroom that has no windows or stationary windows only, it's wise to use a high-capacity ventilation system. The vent system should be capable of exchanging the air eight times per hour.

Large windows admit abundant light in this bathing alcove. The window combination was selected and set to frame the view, effectively bring the countryside into the room. Here, where privacy isn't an issue, window coverings are unnecessary.

CHAPTER 6

Accessories

athroom accessories are not strictly necessary in and of themselves: They're objects that add beauty, convenience, efficiency or effectiveness to the room. From a robe hook beside the tub to a lighted magnifying mirror next to the sink, accessories make daily routines just a little easier, more comfortable, or more enjoyable.

The key to accessorizing is balance: The pieces you choose should make the most of the space without overwhelming it. They should also complement the style and finish of fixtures and fittings in the room.

As you look through the photos in this chapter, think about your bathroom, the family members who use it, and the daily routines. Imagine what would make life more pleasant as you start and end each day. Perhaps you'd like a reading light near the tub or toilet, a stack of baskets to hold hand towels and wash cloths, or even a towel warmer to take the chill off winter mornings. All those things and more are available.

Mirrors, hooks, baskets, storage pieces—they all contribute to the ambience as well as the efficiency of this eclectic bathroom.

Placing the center of the mirror at eye level makes it easy to use.

Well-placed hooks make it easy to keep bathrooms neat and organized.

Bathroom accessories simplify daily living.

Live flowers and green plants freshen and sweeten the air and the atmosphere.

Small lamps add a cozy glow to bathrooms.

Throw rugs absorb water and provide a soft, warm spot for bare feet. They should be slip-resistant and easy to launder.

Baskets keep magazines and other reading material collected and close at hand.

Mirrors multiply the available light, especially when they're placed opposite or adjacent to windows. Here, a generous mirror is positioned to bounce light off the angles of the ceiling and walls, a very clever strategy.

A textured glass panel in the door protects privacy without totally blocking light. It's a lovely touch in this well-lit room, but would be especially welcome in a bathroom without windows.

A small shelf behind the sink is especially useful when counterspace is limited.

Wall-mounted cup holders and soap dishes save precious space in small bathrooms.

Tilted mirrors allow seated or short users to easily see themselves.

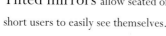

ACCESSORIES

The towel racks match the style and finish of the faucet, light fixtures, and cup brackets.

Brackets hold drinking cups near the sink.

Mirrored medicine cabinets provide handy, easy-to-reach storage space. One caveat regarding this or any other medicine cabinet: Cleaning supplies and medications should always be stored in cool, dry, lockable space.

Adjustable, lighted magnifying mirrors bring delicate grooming tasks into focus. The tiniest details—stray eyebrows, nose hairs, even that bit of spinach between your teeth—are clearly visible in devices like this.

A sturdy bar beneath the counter makes it easy for seated users to pull themselves into position. The bar can hold hand towels and washcloths.

A bathroom should have at least 24" of towel bar for each person who regularly uses it. At least one bar or hook should be positioned within 12" of a shower or tub.

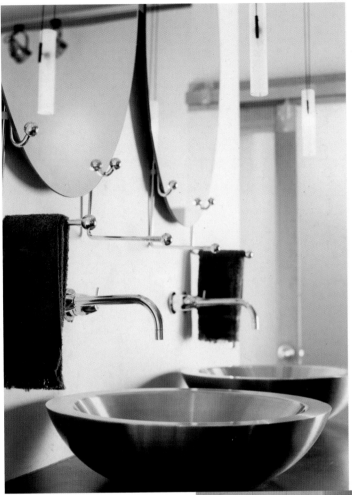

Extensions of the mirror brackets, these towel racks hold towels right where they're needed.

Warm towels may be the ultimate luxury when you step from a shower or tub. Some models must be hard wired and some require plumbing connections, but free-standing, plug-in models are widely available as well.

Whatever style you choose, make sure it's UL listed and properly installed. Free-standing models should be plugged into GFCI-protected outlets.

Transforming vintage pieces into bathroom accessories saves money and makes your bathroom uniquely your own. Replace a tired print with a mirror in a vintage picture frame; hang interesting baskets on the walls to store towels; drape vintage linens over simple rods for window treatments; place a coat rack near the tub to hold towels. Even if your tastes are more contemporary, there's no doubt your attic or storage space contains at least a few pieces that could be repurposed into attractive, useful bathroom accessories.

This plumbing riser extends to support a track for the shower curtain, a very clever arrangement for this free-standing tub. The braces for the riser are secured to studs behind the wood paneling with sturdy anchors.

It might not seem like weight is an issue—after all, it's only a shower curtain. Except it's not just the shower curtain you're supporting. A set-up like this should be prepared to support the weight of someone who uses it to steady himself or grabs it while falling.

Shower curtains can be far more than a ubiquitous plastic panel from the discount store. Many ready-made curtains are made from easy-care fabrics that dry quickly and hold their color well. Backed by a sturdy liner, such curtains can be graciously draped over an attractive curtain rod or standard shower rod.

Free-standing tubs often lack places to keep bathing supplies. Here, a chrome basket neatly solves that problem. The accent table and the chair also provide spaces to keep supplies and comforts.

Recessed light fixtures highlight the tile shower and glass door.

The lines of the mirror frame echo the trim around the shower, integrating the two.

The wooden slats on the shower bench are a subtle but effective coordinating touch.

When counter space is limited, accessories can provide creative solutions. Here, the vanity counter and trough sink are long on style but a bit short on space. A wooden tray effectively divides the sink and provides a place to set toiletries and other grooming necessities.

Using wood to match the vanity makes it clear the tray is part of the design rather than an afterthought.

For those who can't wake up without talk radio or music, audio speakers in the shower are a fantastic choice. These are, of course, special components built to withstand exposure to moisture and heat.

In some circumstances it would be possible to retrofit speakers into a shower, but the best time by far to add them is during new construction or a major remodel. Upper-end designers report that most new bathrooms à la family rooms and home theaters are being wired for sound these days.

*Design*Wise

Lori Jo M. Krengel, CKD, CBD
Kitchens by Krengel, Inc.
St. Paul, MN

- Bathroom mirrors have come a long way in recent years, from anti-fog and magnifying features to TV and computer monitors built into or projected onto the surface.

- When planning for towel bars, don't just mount them in whatever space is available. Rather, consider the size and function of the towel, then install a towel bar large enough to allow towels to be hung to dry properly.

- Towel bars with warmers can act as space heaters in small bathrooms.

- Many homeowners are installing two toilet paper holders at each location for convenience.

ACCESSORIES

(left) **Good design has a starting point, an anchor.** The design of this powder room is based on the unique vessel sink. The color and shape of the mirror, hanging pendants—even the drawer pulls—take their cues from the round shape of the sink. Notice that while the pieces don't precisely match, they clearly were chosen to complement one another.

*Idea*Wise

Reading in the tub isn't always as relaxing as one might hope, what with trying to keep the book out of the water and in a comfortable position. No problem. Keep your books and magazines high and dry with a custom-built bookstand.

Measure the width of your tub, then cut a piece of 3/4" teak about 10 inches wide and long enough to fit across the tub. Cut two 10 × 2" cleats of teak and secure one cleat near each end of the tray, using glue and 1¼" screws. Sand the tray, apply a coat of teak oil, and let the oil dry according to manufacturer's instructions. (You could also purchase a tray to fit across the tub, if you can find one the right size.)

Use silicone caulk to secure a clear acrylic cookbook stand to the tray, about an inch from the front.

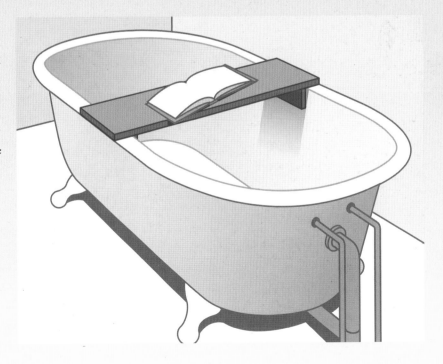

Resource Guide: Kitchens

Introduction

page 6:
cabinets by
Plain & Fancy Custom Cabinetry
Oak Street & Route 501
Schaefferstown, PA 17088
1-800-447-9006
717-949-6571
www.plainfancycabinets.com

page 9:
kitchen design by
Kitchens by Krengel
1688 Grand Avenue
St. Paul, MN 55105
651-698-0844
www.kitchensbykrengel.com

pages 10 and 11:
kitchen design by
**Abruzzo Kitchens/
Jim Dase Kitchen Designer**
1105 Remington Road
Schaumburg, IL 60173
847-885-0500
www.abruzzokitchens.com

Walls, Floors & Ceilings

page 29:
kitchen design by
DeWitt Designer Kitchens
12417 Ventura Boulevard
Studio City, CA 91604
818-505-6901
www.dewittdesignerkitchens.com

page 39 (lower left):
cabinets and kitchen design by
Plain & Fancy Custom Cabinetry
Oak Street & Route 501
Schaefferstown, PA 17088
1-800-447-9006
717-949-6571
www.plainfancycabinets.com

page 17 (above): ceramic tile by
Meredith Tile
P.O. Box 8854
Canton, OH 44711
330-484-1656
www.meredithtile.com

page 17 (below): ceramic tile backsplash by
Ceramic Tiles of Italy
Viale Monte Santo, 40
41049 Sassuolo (MO), Italy
+39 0536 818111
info@assopiastrelle.it
www.italiatiles.com

page 20: concrete countertops by
Buddy Rhodes Studio, Inc.
2130 Oakdale Avenue
San Francisco, CA 94124
877-706-5303
www.buddyrhodes.com

page 21 (both photos):
cabinets by
Plato Woodwork, Inc.
Plato, MN 55370
1-800-328-5924
www.platowoodwork.com

page 23 (above): appliances by
Dacor
1440 Bridge Gate Drive
Diamond Bar, CA 91765
1-800-793-0093
www.dacor.com

page 23 (below): cabinets by
IKEA Home Furnishings
610-834-0180
www.Ikea-USA.com

page 24: TimberGrass Flat Grain
Natural floor by
Teragren LLC
12715 Miller Road Northeast,
Suite 301
Bainbridge Island, WA 98110
206-842-9477
1-800-929-6333
teragren.com

page 26 (above): sheet vinyl floor by Armstrong
Flooring

page 27 (above): hardwood floor by Armstrong
Flooring
Armstrong Flooring
Armstrong World Industries
2500 Columbia Avenue
Lancaster, PA 17603
717-397-0611
www.armstrong.com

page 27 (below): cabinets by
Diamond Cabinets
visit the website to
locate a local dealer
www.diamondcabinets.com

page 28 (below): laminate flooring by
Pergo
Attention: Consumer Affairs
P.O. Box 1775
Horsham, PA 19044-6775
1-800-33-PERGO
(1-800-337-3746)
www.pergo.com

pages 29 and 30 **DeWitt Designer Kitchens**
12417 Ventura Boulevard
Studio City, CA 91604
818-505-6901
www.dewittdesignerkitchens.com

page 31 (left): kitchen design by
Kitchens by Stephanie
3640 Thornapple Drive
Grand Rapids, MI 49546
616-942-9922
www.kitchensbystephanie.com

pages 32 and 33 (left):
cabinets by
Plato Woodwork, Inc.
Plato, MN 55370
1-800-328-5924
www.platowoodwork.com

Storage & Display

page 36:   cabinets by
Mill's Pride
2 Easton Oval, Suite 310
Columbus, OH 43219
1-800-441-0337
Mills Pride cabinets available
exclusively at Home Depot
stores

page 38 (above): cabinets by
Mill's Pride
2 Easton Oval, Suite 310
Columbus, OH 43219
1-800-441-0337
Mills Pride cabinets available
exclusively at Home Depot
stores

page 38 (below): cabinets by
KraftMaid Cabinetry, Inc.
P.O. Box 1055
Middlefield, OH 44062
For more information or to
locate an authorized dealer
near you, call
1-888-562-7744
or go to
www.kraftmaid.com

page 39:   cabinets by
Crown Point Cabinetry
P.O. Box 1560
Claremont, NH 03743
800-999-4994
www.crown-point.com

page 40 (below):   cabinet and drawer
accessories by
Poggenpohl U.S., Inc.
145 U.S. Highway 46 West,
Suite 200
Wayne, NJ 07470
www.poggenpohl.com

page 41 (above and lower right):
cabinet and drawer accessories
available through
Hafele America Co.
336-889-2322
www.hafeleonline

page 41 (lower left):
cabinets and accessories by
Plain & Fancy Custom Cabinetry
Oak Street & Route 501
Schaefferstown, PA 17088
1-800-447-9006
717-949-6571
www.plainfancycabinets.com

page 42 (above):   cabinets by
Plain & Fancy Custom Cabinetry
Oak Street & Route 501
Schaefferstown, PA 17088
1-800-447-9006
717-949-6571
www.plainfancycabinets.com

page 42 (below):   cabinets by
Plato Woodwork, Inc.
Plato, MN 55370
1-800-328-5924
www.platowoodwork.com

page 43:   cabinets by
Dura Supreme
300 Dura Drive
Howard Lake, MN 55349
1-888-711-3872
www.durasupreme.com

page 44:   cabinets by
KraftMaid Cabinetry, Inc.
P.O. Box 1055
Middlefield, OH 44062
For more information or to
locate an authorized dealer
near you, call
1-888-562-7744
or go to
www.kraftmaid.com

page 45:   cabinets by
Dura Supreme
300 Dura Drive
Howard Lake, MN 55349
1-888-711-3872
www.durasupreme.com

pages 46 (below) and 47:
kitchen design by
Kitchens by Krengel
1688 Grand Avenue
St. Paul, MN 55105
651-698-0844
www.kitchensbykrengel.com

page 48:   cabinets by
Plain & Fancy Custom Cabinetry
Oak Street & Route 501
Schaefferstown, PA 17088
1-800-447-9006
717-949-6571
www.plainfancycabinets.com

page 49 (both images):
kitchen design by
Kitchens by Krengel
1688 Grand Avenue
St. Paul, MN 55105
651-698-0844
www.kitchensbykrengel.com

pages 50 and 51 both images; page 52 (above):
cabinets by
Dura Supreme
300 Dura Drive
Howard Lake, MN 55349
1-888-711-3872
www.durasupreme.com

page 52 (below): cabinets by
KraftMaid Cabinetry, Inc.
P.O. Box 1055
Middlefield, OH 44062
For more information or to
locate an authorized dealer
near you, call
1-888-562-7744
or go to
www.kraftmaid.com

pages 53 and 54: countertops by
Cambria Corporation
636 Waverly St.
Palo Alto, CA 94301
650-328-9270
www.cambria.com

page 55 (both images):
kitchen design by
DeWitt Designer Kitchens
12417 Ventura Boulevard
Studio City, CA 91604
818-505-6901
www.dewittdesignerkitchens.com

page 56: kitchen design by
**Sawhill Custom Kitchens &
Design, Inc.**
@ International Market Square
275 Market Street, Suite 157
Minneapolis, MN 55405
612-338-3991
www.sawhillkitchens.com

page 57: concrete countertops by
Buddy Rhodes Studio, Inc.
2130 Oakdale Avenue
San Francisco, CA 94124
877-706-5303
www.buddyrhodes.com

page 60: countertops by
DuPont Corian
offered by fine retailers
everywhere
For further information or to
find a retailer near you, call
1-800-4-CORIAN
(1-800-426-7426)
or go to
www.corian.com
To order samples, go to
www.coriansamples.com

page 61 (both images):
countertops by
Formica Corporation
Formica brand laminate offered
by fine retailers everywhere
For further information or to
find a retailer near you, call
1-800-FORMICA
(1-800-367-6422)
or go to
www.formica.com

Food Preparation & Clean Up

pages 64:   cabinets by
Plain & Fancy Custom Cabinetry
Oak Street & Route 501
Schaefferstown, PA 17088
1-800-447-9006
717-949-6571
www.plainfancycabinets.com

page 67:   cabinets by
KraftMaid Cabinetry, Inc.
P.O. Box 1055
Middlefield, OH 44062
For more information or to
locate an authorized dealer
near you, call
1-888-562-7744
or go to
www.kraftmaid.com

pages 68 and 69: dishwashers by
Asko
AM Appliance Group
P.O. Box 851805
Richardson, TX 75085-1805
For more information or to
find a distributor near you, call
1-800-898-1879 or
972-238-0794
or go to
www.askousa.com

page 70:   cabinets by
IKEA Home Furnishings
610-834-0180
www.Ikea-USA.com

page 73:   countertops by
Buddy Rhodes Studio, Inc.
2130 Oakdale Avenue
San Francisco, CA 94124
877-706-5303
www.buddyrhodes.com

page 74:   countertops by
Formica Corporation
Formica brand laminate offered
by fine retailers everywhere
For further information or to
find a retailer near you, call
1-800-FORMICA
(1-800-367-6422)
or go to
www.formica.com

page 75: sink by
Kohler
Kohler products available at
showrooms and retailers
worldwide
To locate a showroom or
retailer near you, call
1-800-4-KOHLER (456-4537)
or go to
www.us.kohler.com

page 76: cabinets by
Plain & Fancy Custom Cabinetry
Oak Street & Route 501
Schaefferstown, PA 17088
1-800-447-9006
717-949-6571
www.plainfancycabinets.com

pages 78 and 79 (both images):
concrete countertops by
Buddy Rhodes Studio, Inc.
2130 Oakdale Avenue
San Francisco, CA 94124
877-706-5303
www.buddyrhodes.com

page 80: metal tile for backsplash by
Crossville Porcelain Stone
P.O. Box 1168
Crossville, TN 38557
To find an authorized dealer
near you, call
931-484-2110
or go to
www.crossville-ceramics.com

page 82 (above and below):
cabinets by
Plato Woodwork, Inc.
Plato, MN 55370
1-800-328-5924
www.platowoodwork.com

page 83 (above): appliances by
Amana
Amana is a brand in the family
of Maytag Appliances
Maytag Customer Service
403 West 4th Street North
Newton, IA 50208
For information or to locate a
retailer near you, call
1-800-843-0304
or go to
www.amana.com

page 83 (below): ceramic tile by
Daltile
7834 C.F. Hawn Freeway
Dallas, TX 75217
For more information or to
locate a dealer near you, call
214-398-1411
or go to
www.daltileproducts.com

page 84: kitchen design by
Kitchens by Stephanie, Ltd.
3640 Thornapple Drive
Grand Rapids, MI 49546
616-942-9922
www.kitchensbystephanie.com

page 86: appliances by
Amana
Amana is a brand in the family
of Maytag Appliances
Maytag Customer Service
403 West 4th Street North
Newton, IA 50208
For information or to locate a
retailer near you, call
1-800-843-0304
or go to
www.amana.com

page 87: cabinets by
Plato Woodwork, Inc.
Plato, MN 55370
1-800-328-5924
www.platowoodwork.com

Dining & Hospitality

pages 90:   kitchen design by
Kitchens by Krengel
1688 Grand Avenue
St. Paul, MN 55105
651-698-0844
www.kitchensbykrengel.com

pages 92 and 94:   cabinets by
Plato Woodwork, Inc.
Plato, MN 55370
1-800-328-5924
www.platowoodwork.com

page 93:   windows by
Andersen Windows, Inc.
1-800-426-4261
www.andersenwindows.com

page 95:   cabinets, furnishings, and
accessories by
IKEA
To shop, request a catalog, or
find a store near you, call
1-800-434-4532
or go to
www.IKEA.com

page 100 (all images):
kitchen design by
Kitchens by Krengel
1688 Grand Avenue
St. Paul, MN 55105
651-698-0844
www.kitchensbykrengel.com

page 105:   island made of TimberGrass
Flat Grain Natural panels from:
Teragren LLC
12715 Miller Road Northeast
Suite 301
Bainbridge Island, WA 98110
For more information, call
1-800-929-6333 or
206-842-9477
or go to
teragren.com

Lighting

page 111:	lighting fixtures by **Tech Lighting** 7401 North Hamlin Skokie, IL 60076 For more information or to locate a showroom near you, call 847-410-4400 or go to www.techlighting.com
page 112:	concrete countertops by **Buddy Rhodes Studio, Inc.** 2130 Oakdale Avenue San Francisco, CA 94124 877-706-5303 www.buddyrhodes.com
page 113:	cabinets by **KraftMaid Cabinetry, Inc.** P.O. Box 1055 Middlefield, OH 44062 For more information or to locate an authorized dealer near you, call 1-888-562-7744 or go to www.kraftmaid.com
page 114:	windows by **Andersen Windows, Inc.** 1-800-426-4261 www.andersenwindows.com
page 115:	cabinets by **SieMatic** Two Greenwood Square 3331 Street Road Suite 450 Bensalem, PA 19020 For more information or to locate a dealer near you, call 1-888-316-2665 or go to www.siematic.com

Convenience & Communication

page 122:   cabinets by
Plato Woodwork, Inc.
Plato, MN 55370
1-800-328-5924
www.platowoodwork.com

page 125 (below): cabinets, furnishings, and
accessories by
IKEA
To shop, request a catalog,
or find a store near you, call
1-800-434-4532
or go to
www.IKEA.com

Introduction

page 135:
Forma bathtub by:
Jason International
1-800-255-5766
www.jasoninterational.com/

page 136:
Bathroom fixtures and fittings by:
Kohler Co.
1-800-4-KOHLER
www.kohlerco.com

Walls, Floors & Ceilings

page 148 (top):
Concrete tiles by:
Buddy Rhodes Studio, Inc.
San Francisco, CA
877-706-5303
www.buddyrhodes.com

page 152 (below):
Vinyl flooring by:
Armstrong Flooring
Armstrong World Industries
717-397-0611
www.armstrong.com

page 157:
DeWitt Talmadge Beall
Dewitt Designer Kitchens
12417 Ventura Boulevard
Studio City, CA 91604
818-505-6901
www.dewittdesignerkitchens.com

page 158 (both):
Concrete tiles by:
Buddy Rhodes Studio, Inc.
San Francisco, CA
877-706-5303
www.buddyrhodes.com

Storage & Display

page 171:
Pat Currier
Currier Kitchens & Baths
135 Route 101A, Carriage Depot
Amherst, NH 03031
603-883-2407
www.currierkitchens-baths.com

page 175:
Bathroom fixtures and fittings by:
Kohler Co.
1-800-4-KOHLER
www.kohlerco.com

page 185 (below):
Glass tile by:
Crossville, Inc.
931-484-2110
www.crossvilleinc.com

page 186 (below):
Concrete countertop by:
Buddy Rhodes Studio, Inc.
San Francisco, CA
877-706-5303
www.buddyrhodes.com

Resource Guide
(continued)

Fixtures

page 193:
Glass tile by:
Crossville, Inc.
931-484-2110
www.crossvilleinc.com

page 195:
Countertop by:
DuPont Corian
1-800-4-CORIAN
www.corian.com

page 196 (left):
Tile by:
Crossville, Inc.
931-484-2110
www.crossvilleinc.com

page 196 (right):
Italian tile by:
Ceramic Tiles of Italy
212-980-1500
www.italytile.com

page 200-201 (both):
Bathroom fixtures and fittings by:
Kohler Co.
1-800-4-KOHLER
www.kohlerco.com

page 202:
Italian tile by:
Ceramic Tiles of Italy
212-980-1500
www.italytile.com

page 205:
Tile by:
Crossville, Inc.
931-484-2110
www.crossvilleinc.com

page 206 (below):
Concrete panels by:
Buddy Rhodes Studio, Inc.
San Francisco, CA
877-706-5303
www.buddyrhodes.com

page 207:
Italian tile by:
Ceramic Tiles of Italy
212-980-1500
www.italytile.com

pages 208-209:
Tile by:
Crossville, Inc.
931-484-2110
www.crossvilleinc.com

page 212:
Bathroom fixtures and fittings by:
Kohler Co.
1-800-4-KOHLER
www.kohlerco.com

page 213 (below):
Linda Burkhardt
Kitchens & Baths by Linda
771 Montauk Hwy., Suite 2
Montauk, NY 11954
631-668-6806
www.lindaburkhardt.com

page 214 (above):
Shower and countertop by:
DuPont Corian
1-800-4-CORIAN
www.corian.com

page 216:
Italian tile by:
Ceramic Tiles of Italy
212-980-1500
www.italytile.com

page 217 (below):
Bathroom fixtures and fittings by:
Kohler Co.
1-800-4-KOHLER
www.kohlerco.com

page 219 (below):
Bathroom fixtures and fittings by:
Kohler Co.
1-800-4-KOHLER
www.kohlerco.com

Fittings

page 231:
Bathroom fixtures and fittings by:
Jacuzzi
866-234-7727
www.jacuzzi.com

page 233:
Trudy McCollum, ASID, CKD, CBD
Kitchen and Bath Ideas
8800 Maumelle Blvd., Suite B
North Little Rock, AR 72113
501-812-0200
trudy@kitchenandbathideas.biz

Lighting & Ventilation

page 241:
Jeff Livingston, LS
Deborah Foucher Stuke, CLC
Luce Design Group, LLC
PO Box 132
Manchester, NH 03105
603-821-5853
www.lucedesigngroup.com

page 243:
concrete countertop by:
Buddy Rhodes Studio, Inc.
San Francisco, CA
877-706-5303
www.buddyrhodes.com

page 247:
vinyl casement and
transom window unit by:
JELD-WEN
1-800-JELD-WEN
www.jeld-wen.com

Accessories

page 248:
Suntunnel skylight by:
VELUX-America, Inc.
1-800-88-VELUX
www.velux-america.com

page 254 (below):
tilted mirror by:
Ginger
1-888-469-6511
www.gingerco.com

page 260:
concrete countertop by:
Buddy Rhodes Studio, Inc.
San Francisco, CA
877-706-5303
www.buddyrhodes.com

page 261:
Lori Jo Krengel, CKD, CBD
Kitchens by Krengel
1688 Grand Avenue
St. Paul, MN 55105
651-698-0844
www.kitchensbykrengel.com

Additional Resources

National Kitchen and Bath Association
For a free kitchen workbook, remodeling guide, and other helpful information, visit NKBA online at:

> www.nkba.org
> Or call 1-800-843-6522
> You can also write to:
> NKBA
> 687 Willow Grove Street
> Hackettstown, NJ 07840

For reviews, analysis and comparison of kitchen appliances and other consumer goods, go to:

> www.consumersearch.com
> www.goodhousekeeping.com

For buying guides, planning tools and additional how-to information, go to:

> www.homedepot.com
> www.lowes.com

For ideas, products, and advice on kitchen planning and design, go to:

> www.superkitchens.com

For ideas, products, advice on kitchen planning or to locate a kitchen professional near you, go to:

> www.kitchens.com

Photo Credits

p. 4 © iStock/www.iStock.com

p. 6 © iStock/www.iStock.com

p. 9 photo courtesy of Kitchens by Krengel/ photo by Mims Photography

p. 10, 11 Photos courtesy of Abruzzo Kitchens, kitchen design by Jim Dase

p. 13 photo courtesy of Crown Point Cabinetry

p. 14 photo © Neil Kelly

p. 17 photo courtesy of Ikea

p. 18 (top & lower) photos courtesy of Walker Zanger

p. 19 (top) photo courtesy of Meredith Collection; (lower) courtesy of Ceramic Tiles of Italy

p. 20 photo courtesy of Ikea

p. 21 Photos courtesy of Koechel Peterson & Associates for Plato Woodwork, Inc.

p. 22 Beateworks, Inc., © Andrea Rugg / Beateworks.com

p. 23 (top) Photo courtesy of Dacor (www.dacor.com); (lower) courtesy of Ikea

p. 24 (left) Photo courtesy of Teragren, LLC; (right) © Dennis Krukowski

p. 26 (top) Armstrong Flooring; (lower) photo © Douglas Hill / Beateworks.com

p. 27 (top) photo courtesy of Armstrong Flooring; (lower) courtesy of Diamond Cabinets

p. 28 (top) photo courtesy of Armstrong Flooring; (lower) courtesy of Pergo

p. 29, 30 photos courtesy of Dewitt Designer Kitchens

p. 31 (left) photo © David Leale for Kitchens by Stephanie, Ltd.; (right) © Elizabeth Whiting & Associates / Alamy

p. 32 (left:) photos courtesy of Koechel Peterson & Assoc. for Plato Woodwork;

p. 33 (left) photo courtesy of Koechel Peterson & Assoc. for Plato Woodwork; (right) photo © Micheal Arnaud / Beateworks.com

p. 34 photo courtesy of Ikea

p. 36 photo courtesy of Mill's Pride

p. 37 photo courtesy of Diamond Cabinets

p. 38 photo courtesy of Mill's Pride

p. 39 photo courtesy Crown Point Cabinetry

p. 40 (top) photo courtesy of Ikea; (lower) courtesy of Poggenpohl

p. 41: (top left) photo courtesy of Crown Point Cabinetry; (lower left) Plain and Fancy Custom Cabinetry; (top & lower right) Hafele America

p. 42 (top) photo courtesy of Plain and Fancy Custom Cabinetry; (lower) Koechel Peterson & Associates for Plato Woodwork, Inc.

p. 43, 44 photos courtesy of Dura Supreme

p. 45 photo courtesy of Kraftmaid Cabinetry, Inc.

p. 46 (top) photo © Eric Roth; (lower right) courtesy of Kitchens by Krengel, Mims Photography

p. 47 photo courtesy of Kitchens by Krengel, Mims Photography

p. 48 photo courtesy of Plain and Fancy Custom Cabinetry

p. 49 photos courtesy of Kitchens by Krengel

p. 50, 51 photos courtesy of Dura Supreme

p. 52 (top) photo courtesy of Dura Supreme; (lower) Kraftmaid Cabinetry, Inc.

p. 53 photo © Karen Melvin Photography for Cambria Corporation

p. 54 photo © Karen Melvin Photography for Cambria Corporation

p. 55 photos courtesy of Dewitt Designer Kitchens

p. 56 photo © Saari & Forrai Photography for Sawhill Custom Kitchens & Design, Inc.

p. 57 photo courtesy of Buddy Rhodes Studio, Inc.

p. 58 photo © Karen Melvin Photography for Cornelius Interior Design, Minneapolis, MN

p. 59 photo © Karen Melvin for Pappas Design, Minneapolis, MN

p. 60 photo courtesy of DuPont Corian

p. 61 (top) photo courtesy of Formica Corp.; (lower) photo © Shelley Metcalf

Kitchen Index

A

Aisle width, 51
Appliances, 63, 72

B

Backsplash, 18-22, 29, 30, 49, 58, 60, 80, 83, 87, 104
Bamboo flooring, 24, 25
Beadboard, 21, 30, 46, 96
Beams as design element, 16, 31, 33
Blackboard, 127, 128
Booths & banquettes, 44, 93
Brick cladding, 16, 23

C

Cabinets, 21, 34-61, 77, 81
  corners, 41, 42, 45
  framed vs. frameless, 37
  guidelines, 40, 43
  shelves & accessories, 40, 41
Ceiling, 15, 22, 29-33, 117
Clean-up area, 67-75
Color, 16, 22, 28-30, 46-49, 54, 71, 77, 92, 96, 102-104, 115
  and lighting, 110, 118
  contrasting trim, 21, 49, 54, 55
Communication equipment, 120-131
Concrete countertops, 16, 57, 79
Cooktop, 77, 78, 80, 83-85
Cork flooring, 25, 29
Corners, 41, 42, 45
Cost of remodeling & returns, 8
Countertops, 54-61, 71
  as dining space, 97, 100
  color, 21, 22
  extra-deep, 48
  material, 16, 20, 54-61, 79
  measurement guidelines, 54, 65

D

Desk, 121-125, 130
Dining & hospitality, 88-105
Dishwasher, 16, 68, 69, 77

E

Entertainment systems, 126-129

F

Floors, 15, 24-29, 99
Food preparation, 52, 62-87

H

Hardwood flooring, 25, 27

I

Island, 50-53, 56, 65, 67, 77, 81, 87, 100, 104, 105
  lighting, 119
  making movable island, 75
  multi-level, 50, 67, 90

L

Laminate surfaces,
  countertops, 61
  flooring, 25, 28
Lighting, 29, 31, 51, 78, 81, 91, 96, 101, 106-119
  in cabinet, 43, 44, 90, 113, 119

M

Measurement recommendations,
  aisles, 51
  appliance positions, 68, 69, 76, 77, 86
  counters, 48, 54, 65, 76, 77, 84, 101
  eating area, 94, 101
  lighting, 112
  sink, 71
Message board, 127, 128
Microwave, 76, 82, 86

O

Oven, 65, 84-87, 91

P

Patterns, use of in design, 16
Pull-out surfaces, 94, 95, 125

R

Radiant heating mats, 29
Range, 83-87
Refrigerator, 66, 67, 77
Resale value of remodeling, 8
Resource guide, 264-273

S

Sink, 52, 65-75
Skylight, 16, 29, 32, 116
Solid-surface material, 21, 54, 56, 60, 65, 71
Stainless steel, 20, 58, 72
Stone surfaces,
  countertops, 16, 54-56, 59, 86
  flooring, 25, 28

T

Tile surfaces,
  backsplash, 19, 29, 49
  countertops, 55
  flooring, 16, 24, 25, 28
  walls, 23

V

Vent hood, 80-83, 87
Vinyl flooring, 25, 26

W

Walls, 15-23, 29, 87
Window, 47, 65, 114, 119
Wood surfaces, 21
  countertops, 55
  flooring, 25, 27
Work triangle, 64, 90

Bathroom Index

A

Accessibility,
  grab bars, 217, 223
  slip-resistant flooring, 158, 151
  suggestions for, 136–137, 174–175, 194
  tubs and showers, 304–305
Accessories,
  audio speakers, 261
  hooks, 252
  mirrors, 252, 254, 256, 261
  repurposed items, 258
  shelves, 254
  shower curtains, 258, 259
  toilet paper holder, 219
  towel bars and racks, 190, 256-257, 260, 261
  towel warmers, 176, 256, 260
  tub bookstand, 263
  wooden, 179

B

Bathtubs. see: Tubs
Bidets, 218, 222

C

Ceilings, 159–163
Ceramic tile. see: Tile
Concrete, 148, 153, 158, 186, 206
Countertops,
  concrete, 186
  edges for, 180
  glass, 185, 186, 242
  laminates, 171, 180, 181
  solid-surface, 182, 183, 193
  stone, 187
  tile, 184–185
  wood, 187

F

Faucets,
  materials and finishes, 230, 233
  showerheads, 190, 209, 211, 216, 225, 233, 235
  sink, 192, 193, 227, 228, 229, 235
  tub, 204, 205, 231, 232, 233
Floors,
  bamboo, 153
  concrete, 153, 158
  linoleum, 153
  slip-resistance, 143, 151
  stone, 151, 153, 156, 157
  tile, 143, 146, 153, 154, 155, 216
  vinyl, 152, 153
  warming systems, 151, 157, 158
  wood, 153, 159

G

Glass and glass mosaic,
  countertops, 185, 186, 242
  showers, 190, 208, 211, 214
  sinks, 156, 199

H

Heating systems,
  floors, 151, 157, 158
  towel warmers, 176, 257, 260

L

Lighting,
  above showers and tubs, 204, 211, 245
  colors of, 241, 243
  dimmers, 157, 246
  for dressing table, 246
  fluorescent, 241, 242

placement of fixtures, 239, 241, 242
types and combinations, 238–239, 240, 241, 245, 249, 253, 260
windows and skylights, 162–163, 239, 247, 248, 249

M

Medicine cabinets, 145, 159, 171, 255
Mirrors, 242, 246, 252, 254, 255, 256, 261

S

Showers,
  accessible, 216–217
  body spas, 233, 235
  glass walls and doors, 190, 211, 214
  modules, 212, 213, 214
  seats in, 209, 212, 213, 217, 260
  showerheads, 190, 209, 211, 216, 225, 233, 235
  and tub combinations, 201, 213, 234
Sinks,
  console-table, 196
  faucets, 192, 193, 227, 228, 229, 235
  in furniture pieces, 197
  glass, 156, 199
  integral with countertop, 183, 193
  pedestal, free-standing, 193, 194, 213
  self-rimming, 192, 193
  stainless steel, 198
  undermounted, 193, 195, 198, 213
  vessel, 193, 194, 195
  vitreous china, porcelain, 190, 213
  wall-hung, 193, 196
  wooden, 156, 199
Skylights and windows, 162–163, 239, 247, 248, 249
Stone,
  countertops, 187
  floors, 151, 153, 156, 157
  "meshed," 157
  river rocks, 149
  tubs, 207
Storage,
  to add, 172–173
  cabinets, 166, 167, 171, 179
  display, 157, 169, 209
  drawers, shelves, 178, 179
  medicine cabinets, 145, 159, 171, 255
placement of, 168–169, 170, 176–177, 179
  see also: Countertops
Structural support,
  for concrete, 153, 158, 206
  materials for, 144
  for tubs, 141, 201, 202, 205, 206
  for wall-hung sinks, 196

T

Tile,
  ceilings, 160
  countertops, 184, 185
  floors, 143, 146, 153, 154, 155, 216
  grout, 154, 184
  mosaic, 155, 185, 208, 209
  tubs, 207
  versatility and benefits of, 146–147
  walls, 143, 146, 156
Toilets, 218–221, 223
Tubs,
  accessible, 225
  alcove tubs, 200
  deck-mounted, 202, 203, 205
  faucets, 204, 205, 231, 232, 233
  freestanding, 190, 206, 258, 259
  materials for, 199, 201, 206, 207
  and shower combinations, 201, 213, 234
  spa tubs, 202, 204
  structural support for, 141, 201, 202, 205, 206
  for two, 204

U

Universal design. see: Accessibility

V

Ventilation,
  capacity of system, 211, 241, 249
  importance of, 144, 145, 161, 237
  skylights and windows, 239, 247

W

Walls,
  ceramic tile, 143, 146, 156
  concrete, 148
  display niches in, 157, 209
  glass, 190, 211, 214
  painted, 144, 145, 161
  river rock, 149
  wallpaper, 143, 145, 161
  wooden, 150, 159
Windows and skylights, 162–163, 239, 247, 248, 249
Wood,
  accessories, 179
  backsplash and countertops, 172, 187
  ceilings, 159, 192
  floors, 153, 159
  sinks and tubs, 156, 199
  walls, 150, 159

Also From CREATIVE PUBLISHING international

Complete Guide to Attics & Basements

Complete Guide to Bathrooms

Complete Guide Build Your Kids a Treehouse

Complete Guide to Ceramic & Stone Tile

Complete Guide to Creative Landscapes

Complete Guide to Custom Shelves & Built-Ins

Complete Guide to Decks

Complete Guide to Dream Kitchens

Complete Guide to Easy Woodworking Projects

Complete Guide to Finishing Walls & Ceilings

Complete Guide to Floor Décor

Complete Guide to Gazebos & Arbors

Complete Guide to Home Carpentry

Complete Guide to Home Plumbing

Complete Guide to Home Wiring

Complete Guide to Landscape Construction

Complete Guide Maintain Your Pool & Spa

Complete Guide to Masonry & Stonework

Complete Guide to Outdoor Wood Projects

Complete Guide to Painting & Decorating

Complete Guide to Patios

Complete Guide to Roofing & Siding

Complete Guide to Trim & Finish Carpentry

Complete Guide to Windows & Doors

Complete Guide to Wood Storage Projects

Complete Guide to Yard & Garden Features

Complete Outdoor Builder

Complete Photo Guide to Home Repair

Complete Photo Guide to Home Improvement

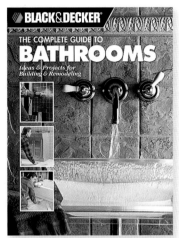

ISBN 1-58923-062-0

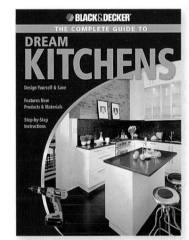

ISBN 1-58923-304-2

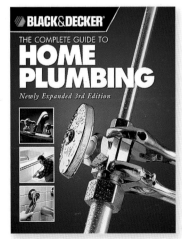

ISBN 1-58923-201-1

Creative Publishing international

400 First Avenue North • Suite 300 • Minneapolis, MN 55401 • www.creativepub.com

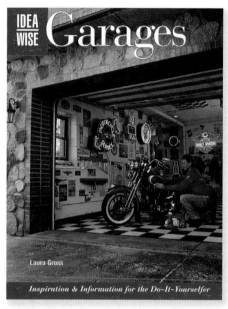
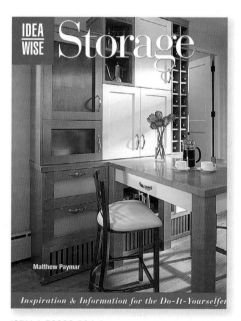